JUDGMENT
IN
PASTORAL
COUNSELING

JUDGMENT
IN
PASTORAL
COUNSELING

LOWELL G. COLSTON

ABINGDON PRESS

Nashville and New York

TO FRANCES

PREFACE

Certainly when one presumes to say something positive about a subject which carries as many negative connotations for many people as does judgment, he is sticking his neck into the proverbial noose. Yet, I feel something must be said in defense of the tremendous impact of judgment on the growth potential of every person. I am reminded of the remark once made by a boyhood chum of mine who, commenting on the preaching of the pastor of our church at that time, said, "He makes the devil sound so real, it scares me. At least I have a pretty good idea who I am against!" Whether or not I have presented judgment that lucidly is to be seen. However, my intent is to show how "taking in" judgment adds wisdom and stature to a man.

This book is basically a report on clinical phenomena which I have observed in over a decade of research in pastoral counseling. The essential germ of the idea was developed into a doctoral dissertation at the University of Chicago. My interest in expanding and reworking the concepts which grew out of the study of the context of pastoral counseling in the Bryn Mawr Community Church in Chicago and the Counseling Center of the University of Chicago, and published, with Seward Hiltner, in *The Context of Pastoral Counseling,* has been stimulated by a recent ground swell of writings dealing with related themes, especially that of responsibility. Writers such as Erik Erikson (*Insight and Responsibility*), Joseph Fletcher (*Moral Responsibility*), William Glasser (*Reality Therapy*), H. Richard Niebuhr (*The Responsible Self*), and O. Hobart Mowrer (*Morality and Mental Health*) have produced variations on the theme of responsibility.

I am dealing with judgment, especially as it is seen in pastoral counseling relationships. Responsibility implies the function of judgment and, although not often expressly stated, it is presumed throughout this discussion.

The function of judgment in pastoral counseling is considered in this book in response to three implied questions: What is the nature of judgment? What are the dynamics of judgment in the counseling relationship? What are the sources of judgment in the context of pastoral counseling?

Part I is intended to form an answer to the first question, stating the specific senses in which the term "judgment" is understood in relation to the particular framework developed herein.

The major thesis of the book is contained in Part II, which is directed to the second question. It describes a clinically observed process which I have called "the assimilation of judgment," and exhibits the actual stages in the struggle of persons to discern and to incorporate the judgment which they experience in relation to themselves, to others, and to God.

The third question follows logically from the first two:

Whence comes the judgment which contributes to personal growth? Since this book puts the issue in the framework of pastoral counseling, the discussion of that question is limited to an explication of sources of judgment within the pastoral context—primarily the pastor and the church, in the sense of the particular community to whom the pastor is responsible.

I owe a debt of gratitude to many people who have contributed indirectly and to a large number who have helped directly with the preparation of this book. My former teacher and colleague, Seward Hiltner, gave me much counsel and encouragement in the original study out of which the basic ideas for the book have come. I am grateful to Mrs. James B. Alexander, Mrs. Jack Daniel, and Mrs. Sandra McMahan for help on the manuscript. My special thanks goes to Mrs. Walter Cardwell for her excellent assistence in getting this manuscript into final form.

Lowell G. Colston

Christian Theological Seminary
Indianapolis, Indiana

CONTENTS

PART III

PART I

I   Judgment and Love

Judgment and love are interrelated concepts. They are mutually supportive and corrective. Therefore, they are concepts which are equally germane to any discussion of pastoral counseling. The centrality of love as the positive dynamic in all human relationships is generally presupposed in literature on the subject. Whether the writer is a psychiatrist, such as William Glasser ("the need to love and be loved and the need to feel that we are worthwhile to ourselves and to others" [1]), or a theologian like Paul Tillich ("the transcendent character of the ultimate source of moral demands—love under the dominance of *agape*" [2]), love as the creative force in human relations is affirmed. The perspective may differ, but the basic affirmation is the same.

Love includes and transcends the other central concept— judgment. As Tillich has pointed out in his remarkable essay on *Morality and Beyond*, "Love, in the sense of *agape*, contains justice in itself as its unconditional element and as its weapon against its own sentimentalization." [3] Thus, love and judgment are mentioned together because they belong

[1] William Glasser, *Reality Therapy* (New York: Harper & Row, 1965), p. 9.
[2] Paul Tillich, *Morality and Beyond* (New York: Harper & Row, 1963), p. 42.
[3] *Ibid.*, p. 39.

together. Judgment is the specific explication of the conditions of love or the conditions under which the principle of love is actualized. Consequently, judgment must not be seen as violating but as fulfilling love.

Joseph Fletcher would go even further in his elaboration of the idea, stating, "Love and justice are the same thing." He decries the low state into which the word "love" has fallen. "But I have another recommendation," he says. "The *best practice is never to use the word 'love'* in Christian ethical discourse. Every time we think 'love' we should *say* 'justice.' For justice has not been hopelessly sentimentalized, or romanticized, or individualized. Not only *is* it Christian love but, as communication, it *says* it. It says what the Biblical *agape* means." [4]

Although I am in fundamental agreement with Fletcher's view, I must confess I am one of the hopeless romanticists who will suffer twinges of sadness at losing "love" from the saying which has had considerable meaning to me: "You shall be just to the Lord your God with all your heart, mind, and soul, and you shall be just to your neighbor as to yourself." Undoubtedly, this *says* what is required, but something seems to be lost in the substitution. I contend it is not just the sentiment, either, but an indication of a fundamental commitment to a relationship.

While I certainly agree with Fletcher's assertion regarding the distortions of the concept of love, I prefer a reappropriation of its essential meaning. Here I follow Tillich's inclusive understanding of the relationship between love and justice.

Conflict occurs, Tillich has shown, when a creature "violates the structure of justice and so violates love itself."

[4] Fletcher, *Moral Responsibility* (Philadelphia: The Westminster Press, 1967), p. 57.

When this happens—and it is the character of creaturely existence that it happens universally—judgment and condemnation follow. . . . Condemnation is not the negation of love but the negation of the negation of love. . . . Judgment is an act of love which surrenders that which resists love to self-destruction.[5]

Tillich sees the "wrath of God" experience as the "awareness of the self-destructive nature of evil." The acts and attitudes of creatures which tend to separate them from the "ground of their being" are experienced as judgment. Thus judgment is interpreted as the experiencing of self-destruction and utter despair. In its condemnatory aspect it is such an experience, but it is more than that. Literally, judgment affirms that which creates and gives hope to the self.

Judgment, therefore, devolves upon relationships. Any expression of justice which views persons with cool detachment is out of context and virtually a contradiction in essential understanding. To relate to another person in love is already to insert a dimension of judgment. It is to say, in effect, "I believe you are worth my attention," or, "I am addressing you and am expecting a response from you," or some other positive or negative judgmental attitude toward the other person. Recognizing that the assumption here is subjective in its essential thrust, we must agree with Tillich that "mere objectivity never occurs between human beings." [6] Justice when taken into love carries with it involvement. This does not mean that judgment is not fair-minded, but precisely so; not operating out of solemn dis-

---

[5] *Systematic Theology* (Chicago: University of Chicago Press, 1951), I, 283.

[6] *Morality and Beyond*, p. 38.

17

regard for one party or another to a relationship, but out of profound regard for both.

The Meaning of Judgment

In popular thought the word "judgment" usually has a negative connotation. It is often equated with condemnation. Any such overidentification of the term with its negative pole obscures its full meaning. Like its correlative term "criticism," judgment refers to the act of being discerningly perceptive about what is both positive and negative. In fact, judgment is derived from the Latin words *ius* ("right") and *dicere* ("to speak"), meaning, literally, "to speak or say right." It is "the condition of right speaking," or "the act of saying what is right." In view of what we have already said regarding the mutuality of love and judgment, with the latter being included in the former, we would say, judgment means to speak in such a way as to affirm the being of others, to create relationships and to re-create those who are involved in them. This is the basic point of view presented herein.

Dictionary definitions of judgment will introduce three variations of meanings which we will consider: (1) "the mental act of judging; the operation of the mind, involving comparison and discrimination, by which knowledge of values and relations is mentally formulated"; (2) "the ability to judge, make a decision, or form an opinion objectively, authoritatively, and wisely, especially in matters affecting action";[7] (3) "the mandate or sentence of God as the judge of all." [8]

[7] *The Random House Dictionary of the English Language*, the unabridged ed. (New York: Random House, 1966).

[8] *Webster's New International Dictionary of the English Language*, 2nd ed. (Springfield, Mass.: G. & C. Merriam Co., 1960).

The first of the definitions describes a phenomenon which is going on continually in persons whose capacity for judging is not in some way impaired or damaged through injury or illness. The person's every move is predicated upon acts of judgment, in which he is deciding among values which may be in fundamental conflict with each other. Such decisions affect his relationships with people as well as with other factors in his environment.

Any meeting of one person with another inevitably involves both persons in judgment. The degree of judgment depends upon the significance or importance of each to the other. The self-esteem and self-respect of each person hang in the balance. The confrontation involves risk. If the positive regard of the other is highly valued, one's vulnerability to judgment is increased and the risk to his self-regard is greater. In this manner one measures his "worthiness." How he is valued by a person or group of persons is crucial. How he values himself both affects this process and is affected by it.

Intensive encounter of one person by another is in itself an act of judgment. Whether the one encountered be a worthy opponent, a valued companion, or a "diamond in the rough," there is a challenge in the engagement. The engagement may be an act of moving against or moving with the other person. Judgment is in both actions, and the worthiness of the other is implied. If the encounter is an intellectual engagement, for example, each will show fundamental respect for the intellect of the other, or the encounter soon will break down.

Judgment as decision is an act of differentiation, serving the essential function of bringing order out of chaos. It establishes the termination point or "closure" which gives unity and organization to existence. It is a creative act.

Decision means cutting off alternative courses of action for the sake of that which is judged to be appropriate, relevant, and integrative in its long-term consequences.

However, if judgment is to be not merely a prudential matter, but a totally responsible one, it will be refined by the judgment of God. The ground for any decision therefore is "love under the dominance of *agape*." That the apostle Paul understood this dimension well is made palpably clear in his letter to the Romans: "O the depth of the riches and wisdom and knowledge of God! How unsearchable are his *judgments* and how inscrutable his ways! 'For who has known the mind of the Lord, or who has been his counselor?' " (Rom. 11:33-34.)

God's judgments are indeed unsearchable and inscrutable, but unless the apostle was immediately aware of them, how could he speak of their quality? What led him to affirm the depth of "the riches and wisdom" of God? His personal experience had taught him the futility of sealing himself off from the persistent "goads" which pricked him into consciousness of the holiness of God and struck him down with the utter realization of the true nature of integrity.

God's judgment is against the pretentiousness and imperialism of man's judgment. He "cuts man down to size" —not to humiliate him or deprecate him but to prompt him to become abundantly and responsibly human. In other words, judgment is made necessary by man's contrariness; and made possible by God's love. The author of the words we quoted above also wrote the famous thirteenth chapter of the first letter to the Corinthians.

Carroll Wise has said, "God does not pronounce judgment for its own sake, but . . . it serves the purpose of His redemptive love," [9] I certainly am in basic agreement with him at this point. However, I have difficulty reconciling the first part of his statement—"the Christian understanding is that judgment belongs to God, not to man" [10]—with the apostle Paul's assertions in several of his letters to the churches. As I will show in a subsequent chapter, he assumed and even recommended that members in the church judge each other. At the same time, he was sharp in his denunciation of those who judge irresponsibly.

Judgment may not "belong" to man, as Wise declares, but man does indeed judge. This is the nature of his freedom. The important questions are: How does he judge? Does he acknowledge that his proximate judgments are under the ultimate judgment of God?

For our purposes of analysis, then, judgment is interpreted as the act of the self judging itself, the self giving and receiving judgment in relation to others, and the self giving and receiving judgment in relation to God. The function of judgment in each instance is to develop the spirit of wisdom and prudence enabling one to know and to discern what is truly creative in attitude and action, to become discriminating as to good and evil, right and wrong, and to be directed toward what is ultimately fulfilling.

---

[9] Wise, *The Meaning of Pastoral Care* (New York: Harper & Row, 1966), p. 81.
[10] *Ibid.*

2 Judgment in the Gospel

Judgment is at the heart of the gospel. This should be stated categorically at the outset. "The concept of judgment cannot be taken out of the New Testament Gospel. It cannot even be removed from the centre to the periphery. Proclamation of the love of God always presupposes that all men are moving towards God's judgment and are hopelessly exposed to it." [1] If the word "hopelessly" is taken to mean "without hope," then possibly either the word "inescapably" or the word "inevitably" should be substituted. Nevertheless, this is precisely the point of view with which we began.

Of course, judgment which is blindly censorious or hypocritical is roundly denounced in the Gospels. Likewise, pious judgments glibly made from a position of non-involvement (the Pharisee's attitude toward the woman in his house in Luke 7:39) are graciously but firmly exposed for their pridefulness and countered with a loving response.

The familiar saying "Judge not, that you be not judged. For with the judgment you pronounced you will be judged" (Matt. 7:1-2) precedes a statement which obviously places the admonition in the context of self-righteous

---

[1] Gerhard Kittel and G. Friedrich, eds. *Theological Dictionary of the New Testament* (Grand Rapids: Eerdmans, 1964), III, 941.

judgment: "Why do you see the speck that is in your brother's eye, but do not notice the log that is in your own eye?" (Matt. 7:3.) One may seek to relieve his own feelings of guilt by working to get the "speck" out of his brother's eye. Yet if his judgment does not take cognizance of his own "log," it lacks true authority. It is judgment flying false colors and is doomed by the very judgment wherein it is judged.

Explicit statements regarding the positive function of judgment are notably missing from the Gospels. But implicitly, either positive or negative judgment is in every encounter of Jesus with persons, with the disciples, and between the disciples and those to whom they ministered. "Woe to you, scribes and Pharisees, hypocrites," Jesus was quoted to have cried in scathing denunciation of the haughty judgments of those groups. Not all his judgments were this severe, and certainly not all were censorious.

The authority in Jesus' confrontation of persons was that of love which included justice—the justice born of profound sensitivity to relationships. An informed and perceptive regard for the person preceded his action toward the person. Thus his challenges "take up your bed and walk" or "go and sin no more" were judgmental in that they were discerning and discriminative of the disciplinary needs of the particular persons involved. He was expected to be an authority, and he acted authoritatively. However, his was not an authority ignorant of the particular psychodynamics of the person he encountered or of the true complexity of the situation to which he addressed himself.

He continually made manifest his profound respect for the person, but he persistently challenged the person to move from where he was to a new level of spirit. A self-

23

satisfied person was told to "go sell what you possess and give it to the poor"; a defensive person was commanded to "come down" from the tree where he had lodged himself. In neither case was the man condemned for being prideful or defensive. In the former encounter, the man was firmly challenged to demonstrate his goodness, and in the latter, the man was called out of his cowering preoccupation with face-saving operations.

Judgment based on *agape* is self-authenticating. "You judge by worldly standards," Jesus was quoted as saying in the Gospel of John. "I pass judgment on no man, but if I do judge, my judgment is valid because it is not I alone who judge, but I and he who sent me" (John 8:15-16 NEB). Despite the pretentious sound of this claim, it is really not self-justifying but is establishing the true ground for authority in judgment. Jesus' reported words reflect the spirit in which his confrontation of any man is to be understood. His is a derived authority for judgment, but only if judgment is appropriate and necessary. He is not trying to prove anything. The ultimate test of his authority is its authenticity. This is not argued rationally or established polemically, but is wholly manifest in attitude and actions.

Two New Testament words commonly translated "judgment" are *krino* and *krisis*. Three English words perhaps best catch the sense that is conveyed in these Greek terms: *confrontation, critique,* and *crisis.* These actually follow a logical sequence in the judgment process.

The first level of judgment in interpersonal relationships, confrontation, is the face-to-face encounter of one with the other in which an address is made and a response is expected. The second level, that of "critique," represents the evaluating of the other person which inevitably takes place in the encounter. The "crisis" level is eventuated when the other's evaluation of one's attitude and behavior sharply contrasts with his own. For the sake of maintaining the relationship, he may consider whether he will try to change the other's perception of his behavior, by agreement or otherwise, or try to change his behavior to win the approval of the other.

We shall now take up the three concepts in order, showing their usages in the New Testament and their applicability to our main concern.

Judgment as Confrontation and Encounter

The idea of "confrontation" is suggested in the Greek word *krino*, as it appears in the following passage: "Do not judge superficially, but be just in your judgments (*krinate*)." (John 7:24 NEB.) If the latter phrase be paraphrased as "be just in your *confrontations*," the sense of what we are conveying may be given. The rather overworked term "dialogue" is also meant here. One cannot truly enter into dialogue or really *confront* another if his judgments are allowed to remain superficial. Conversely, judgments are not just if deep confrontation does not occur.

In fact, this is the only way we can discover what is just, right, true, honorable. "Christ's cardinal principle is that he will not and cannot give us a code of rigid and unalterable rules, applicable in all circumstances in which we find ourselves." [2] Through confrontation and dialogue we open ourselves to each other and to the Spirit of God, so that our spirits are disciplined to carry out a higher ordinance. We are thus admonished to become

[2] *Interpreter's Bible* (Nashville: Abingdon Press, 1952), VIII, 585.

"non-prejudgmental," wherein *our* customs and patterns of living are not absolutized as principle and *our* conventions as eternal and unalterable laws of God. Confrontation means "standing over against," not in the sense of thwarting or frustrating, but in the sense of facing up to oneself and the other.

The human propensity in the face of confrontation of any sort is to hide or cover up. One of the prevailing human fears is to be found out. The shame dynamism begins operating as early as a person becomes aware of the consequences of his behavior. The Adamic myth witnesses to the universality of this phenomenon. Adam and Eve were not only ashamed of their own nakedness in the presence of God, but they tried to maintain their innocence by shifting responsibility from themselves. One may say, it is only one step from the "shame" dynamism to the "blame" dynamism. These operations are at the root of scapegoating, which is a way of reducing anxiety over guilt by shifting blame from one's self or group to another.

Face-to-face confrontation is essential to a productive counseling relationship. Yet covering up is a common reaction. The presented problem is usually somewhat like the "lily pad on the pond" connected in intricate ways with a maze of interrelated roots underneath. The main stem is the prevailing theme of one's preoccupation which is quite likely under the surface, carefully concealed. Often the person is keenly aware of his hiding tactics; often he is not.

A pastor recently reported to me the following part of the first interview he had with a twenty-year-old woman, whose fictitious name is Mavis. She was a college student who had decided to drop out of school for a year to "build up some financial reserves for continuing college." She

26

was visiting relatives in the town where the pastor was located. With Mavis' permission, her aunt called the pastor and arranged an appointment with him for Mavis. Mavis opened the interview by telling the pastor she was having difficulty getting along with people and was concerned about her increasing tendency to withdraw from social contacts. She was talking in vague generalities, and the pastor was getting uncomfortable. Finally, he said to her, "Was it your idea to come here?" She looked at him intently for a moment, then with an embarrassed laugh replied, "No, frankly it wasn't. If I had made the appointment, I probably wouldn't have shown up. That's the way I do things. Since my aunt made it, I figured I'd better come."

"You don't trust your own initiative?" the pastor responded.

"No, you see, if somebody else does it for me, I'll follow through, but if I do it, I usually don't."

For a brief period of time, they discussed her inability to make decisions.

Finally, she said to the pastor, "To be honest with you, I came to you primarily to see if you could recommend a psychiatrist to me. I've seen plenty of psychologists and ministers in regular counseling, but I need someone to challenge me—to not let me get away with keeping things to myself. I know it sounds silly, but I think I've got to have that—if I'm going to get anywhere."

The pastor interpreted her comment to mean that she had sized him up quickly in the early part of the interview and had decided he probably would not really *confront* her effectively. She had apparently decided she could outmaneuver him but did not really wish to get away with it. Some hint of her perception of his reaction was given in

27

her final comment before she left, after he had indeed arranged for her to see a psychiatrist. Obviously seeking to apply some salve to his wounded ego, she said, "Anyway I've told you as much in these few minutes as I've told my other counselors in all the time I have been seeing them."

The young woman was at least cognitively aware of her dependency patterns. Theoretically she could even affirm they must be effectively broken. At the same time she was aware that she must feel the strength of the counselor in his confrontation of her, although she made every effort to avoid it.

The pastor came into direct encounter with Mavis when he put the question to her regarding her expectations of him. She tried to maneuver out of the encounter by agreeing with his perception and then promptly retreating into her defensiveness.

Mavis was searching for a "worthy opponent." She undoubtedly felt her own self-worth would be thus enhanced. On the one hand, she desired to cling and hold on; on the other, she felt she must be pushed firmly but gently away and forced to stand on her own feet. She was asking for the discipline she admittedly "fought so hard against," as she told him at one point, because she regarded it as necessary to the establishment of her own authority.

Judgment as Critique and Discipline

The sense of *krino* as critique is suggested in Paul's statement to the Corinthians: "Is it not those inside the church whom you are to judge (*krinete*)?" (I Cor. 5:12.) He was attacking the Corinthians for their hypocrisy in dissociating from immoral men outside the church, while permitting immorality within the church. This inconsistency in behavior was called sharply to their attention. The Corinthians could not ignore it but were forced to deal with it.

Paul seemed to take for granted the practice of judging a fellow Christian's behavior. "I wrote to you in my letter not to associate with immoral men," he said, "not at all meaning the immoral of this world" (I Cor. 5:9, 10). And later he made his statement stronger: "Drive out the wicked person from among you" (I Cor. 5:13). In regard to legal disputes, he said, "Can it be that there is no man among you wise enough to decide between members of the brotherhood?" (I Cor. 6:5). Addressing the Galatians, Paul again stated the need for judgment in love: "Brethren, if a man is overtaken in any trespass, you who are spiritual should restore him in a spirit of gentleness" (Gal. 6:1).

However, Paul continually warned against hypocrisy in making judgments. "You therefore have no defense— you who sit in judgment, whoever you may be," he warns, "for in judging your fellow-man you condemn yourself, since you, the judge, are equally guilty" (Rom. 2:1 NEB).

Elaboration of the theme "judge not that you be not judged" is evident again in discussion of the practice of religion in the letter of James. "Brothers, you must never disparage one another. He who disparages a brother or passes judgment on a brother disparages the law and judges the law. . . . There is only one lawgiver and judge, the One who is able to save life and destroy it. So who are you to judge your neighbour?" (Jas. 4:11-12 NEB).

In one instance we have seen, Paul, detecting an arrogant and unrepentant attitude, insisted that the Christian community be judgmental to the point of dissociating from an errant brother. On the other hand, he continually warned against the imperiousness and pretentiousness of judgments against one's fellowman. Although judgment for the sake of order within the fellowship was assumed justified, such judgment is always under divine judgment, and all law is ultimately under judgment of the divine Lawgiver.

The word *kritikos* actually appears in Hebrews 4:12 in reference to the judging character of the word of God. "For the word of God is living and active, sharper than any two-edged sword piercing to the division of soul and spirit, of joints and marrow, and discerning (*kritikos*) the thoughts and intentions of the heart." Exposure to the word of God discloses true intentionality. In such encounter the discernment of motives takes place. The critique occurs within the ultimate relationship: "And before him no creature is hidden, but all are open and laid bare to the eyes of him with whom we have to do" (Heb. 4:13).

Judgment as discipline is seen in the Matthean account of Jesus' teaching his disciples: "If your brother sins against you, go and tell him his fault, between you and him alone. If he listens to you, you have gained your brother. But if he does not listen, take one or two others along with you, that every word may be confirmed by the evidence of two or three witnesses. If he refuses to listen to them, tell it to the church; and if he refuses to listen even to the church, let him be to you as a Gentile and a tax collector." (Matt. 18:15-17.) Undoubtedly this was a reflection of the thought and practice of the early church, because it does not accord with Jesus' attitude toward either Gentiles or tax collectors. Nevertheless, it shows the patient effort to effect reconciliation between an offending brother and his accuser recommended in the early church.

Judgment as Crisis and Decision

The turning point in a series of events is called "crisis." Altered circumstances may render the current pattern of organization and conduct of a person irrelevant or even impossible. He can no longer maintain his present course with impunity or without incurring great risk to his very being. Certainly, if he ignores the alarm which has signaled the crisis, he faces the consequences of the danger in continuing on his way. Let us assume that his pattern of living has been to take adavantage of the good graces of a person who is significant to him. That person decides to put the brakes on the "gravy train," and tells the offender where to get off. This is crisis. Either he must take steps to revise his attitude and action or hazard the possibility of alienation and estrangement.

The Greek word *krisis*, from whence comes "crisis," is translated "judgment" in the New Testament. Literally, it means: "a parting," "a separation," "estrangement," "a conflict." Thus, the course of life for a person separates into alternative routes of possible action. He is forced to make a choice or let a decision be made by default, in which case others decide for him.

The experiencing of crisis of some kind or other at some time or other is such a common occurrence to people that it hardly needs further explanation. Almost anyone can recount recent events which have represented crises for him. The crisis is a "growth point"—an opportunity for the person to increase his knowledge of the world and of himself.

Judgment as crisis occurs when the deeds of a person come into the light of justice and truth. The term *krisis* appears in the context of the much quoted John 3:16 passage:

For God so loved the world that he gave his only Son, that whoever believes in him should not perish but have eternal life. For God sent the Son into the world, not to condemn the world (*ou ton kosmon krine*), but that the world might be saved through him. He who believes in him is not condemned (*krinetai*); he who does not believe is condemned already, because he has not believed in the name of the only Son of God. *And this is the judgment (krisis), that the light has come into the world, and men loved darkness rather than light, because their deeds were evil.* For every one who does evil hates the light, and does not come to the light, lest his deeds should be exposed. But he who does what is true comes to the light, that it may be clearly seen that his deeds have been wrought in God. (John 3:16-21, italics mine.)

The meaning is clear. *Krisis* is the world judgment of Christ. This is not a future judgment, it is present already. Christ's coming into the world occasions crisis or judgment.

The notion of separation is hinted here, but it is not separation in the sense of alienation. The crisis precipitated in the act of God's love through Christ is separation as "differentiation"—the distinction between the deeds which glorify God, thus consummate human fulfillment and those which indulge the self but which are evil in their long range consequences. Of greater importance, however, is the separation in terms of relationship. The contrast between the holiness of Christ and the sinfulnes of man brings crisis, but it is not condemnation, unless a man choose to exclude himself by not accepting Christ.

Crisis or judgment is eventuated in the exposure of what is being hidden or concealed. The public official who misappropriates funds by juggling the books "hates the light" which shows up his misdeeds. Anyone who tries to let "darkness" cover his exploits of self-aggrandizement faces the possible crisis effected through the revealing light of truth.

The popular appeal of the passage of scripture we have quoted is understandable because it states a central thesis of the Christian gospel—that judgment is in the context of love. The application of this theme to the pastoral ministry will be explicated further in a subsequent chapter. Suffice it to say now that preaching and worship not only communicate the grace but also the judgment of God. It is easy enough to say that crisis is for one's own good. Nevertheless, it is true. The judgment of God flows from his love. It is the confrontation which calls us into responsible relationship with him.

Without crisis reconciliation is not possible. The one who can resolutely face the gaze of the judge, not in sneering defiance or sullen compliance, but in eye-to-eye, honest confrontation, is in the process of becoming reconciled—to others and to himself. If he avoids the light of the countenance of the other, he stands condemned by his own choice. He elects not to enter into relationship with the other.

In counseling and psychotherapy the person's cover-up tactics may be so cleverly and persistently maintained that a crisis may have to be provoked. However, if the pastor presumes to instigate a crisis, he will do well to assess carefully his willingness and his ability to endure it with the person. Responsibility is as incumbent upon the pastor as upon the person he counsels.

It should be made clear at this point that the assimilation of judgment, a process which we will discuss later, presupposes crisis. Formal counseling is actually based on the assumption that therapy has already begun. The first step, recognition that something is wrong and that to some degree the trouble is within oneself, has presumably already been taken. True, the person may not really understand his own motivations for going to the pastor, but that he is aware of crisis on some level may be assumed. Further crises undoubtedly will be encountered or even engendered in the counseling relationship.

Judgment as decision is demanded in every instance of crisis. It is not a "one-time thing," but is necessitated when the true complexity of any issue is faced. The man "in Christ" Paul noted, for example, is not free from judgment, but is actually under greater judgment. He is committed to a relationship in which "much is given, but also much is required." His true fulfillment comes in the assumption of the greater responsibility to discipline himself and others to be worthy "heirs of the promise," faithful and diligent sons of God. Such commitment is not without pain, frustration, suffering, and disappointment. But integrity in relationship to God once prompted a decision which even destined a cross!

Three manifestations of judgment have been noted: confrontation, critique, and crisis. We have seen how these are derived from the Greek terms *krino* and *krisis*, and that they receive their authority from the relationships in which they occur.

These factors may be seen operating in the interpersonal process in the following ways: *confrontation* is the act of facing the person where he is in this moment of his existence; *critique* is the process of helping him evaluate his personal strengths and weaknesses and provoking the *crisis,* which his self-awareness brings and which is his opportunity for growth.

We will turn to the next in the sequential order of factors in the function of judgment—that which I have called the assimilation process. This is the point at which counseling usually begins. Counseling presupposes confrontation, critique, and crisis. These are the prior order of business in activating the personal growth potential.

3 The Assimilation
of
Judgment

There are two basic modes of responding to judgment:
(1) developing multifarious patterns of avoiding, denying,
or trying to escape it, or (2) taking it into oneself or
"assimilating" it. The latter mode is essential to growth.
Judgment is given to stimulate creativity. The assimilation
of judgment gives structure to what is being created.

Defensive Reactions to Judgment

Among the typical defensive reactions to judgment
are: denial of its reality through escape into fantasy,
wishful thinking; projection of blame on others; avoidance (perhaps through attempts at compensation for that
of which the judgment makes one aware); internalization
of the judgment (thus not dealing with the external realities it signifies); withdrawal, appealing to others for sym-
pathy, etc.; the development of symptoms which excuse
one from having to face the judgment of which he is
aware; repression, which gives rise to "free-floating" anxiety and an undifferentiated awareness of judgment which
one fears would be overwhelming; rationalization or intel-
lectualization through which the person tries to talk himself
or someone else out of the necessity for change in the di-

rection the judgment points; "acting out" in some way which will convince the person himself he has "done something" in regard to what the judgment is about, but not taking responsible action appropriate to positive, long-range goals involved in the judgment.

All these reactions to judgment tend to abort the process of assimilation of judgment. They are efforts to escape rather than assimilate judgment. Yet, one cannot actually escape judgment, and although he may deceive himself into believing he can erect and maintain his often intricate systems of defense, he quickly finds he cannot seal himself off from judgment.

Guilt Reactions to Judgment

The realization of the inadequacy of his deceptiveness, evasiveness, etc., is experienced affectively as guilt. Lewis Sherrill has shown that guilt may be seen as "fact," "feeling," or a combination of the two. Guilt as "fact" implies "one has done something forbidden or failed to do something required." "As feeling, 'guilt' refers to the emotional aspect of the experience of one who stands in judgment upon himself and condemns himself or at least acknowledges others' condemnations of himself as deserved." [1] These two categories do not lend themselves easily to rational analysis. For this reason, Sherrill has suggested that, to understand them, we must go beyond the rational to the level of feelings.

One cannot do justice to a discussion of guilt without a prior consideration of anxiety, which is basic to understanding guilt. A reinterpretation of a Freudian model may

[1] Sherrill, *Guilt and Redemption* (Richmond: John Knox Press, 1945), p. 62.

be helpful at this point. Diagrammatically, the sequence is shown as follows:

Observed threat—anxiety—hostility—guilt.

As Paul Tillich has shown, the anxiety reaction to a perceived threat may be "ontological" or "existential," when the threat is in some aspect of existence itself, or "pathological," when the threat is "the consequence of the failure of the self to take the anxiety upon itself." [2] In any event, hostile reactions to the anxiety experienced arouse feelings of guilt. One feels guilty over the resultant separation and estrangement.

The assimilation of judgment is the act of differentiating what one is anxious about and taking appropriate action to deal with it. "Appropriate action" includes developing creative attitudes toward ontological anxiety, on the one hand, and rejecting avoidance and denial patterns in favor of self-affirming actions toward taking judgment into the self, on the other.

Although my fundamental position bears resemblance to the views of O. H. Mowrer, I reject the Pelagian[3] tendencies implied in his assumptions. He asserts, "In psychopathology guilt is real rather than illusory ("delusional"). . . . In the therapeutic situation (it) is not mere understanding and insight (in the Freudian sense of these terms) but a changed, repentant view of oneself—and—contrition

[2] Tillich, *The Courage to Be* (New Haven: Yale University Press, 1952), p. 77.

[3] Pelagius decried the low tone of morals in the Christian community of his day. He believed this was due largely to a lack of a vivid sense of personal responsibility. Religiously and theologically he took a view which was at the opposite pole from Augustine, who was skeptical regarding man's capacity for moral regeneration.

and confession must be followed by meaningful, active forms of atonement or restitution." [4] I see all these factors as integral to the assimilation process. But I do not see insight or understanding as of less importance than active forms of atonement. Furthermore, one cannot possibly make full restitution for the guilt which arises from existential anxiety. Granted that some "closure" is needed in relation to the potentially overwhelming character of guilt, we cannot imply that *all* guilt can be overcome through restitution.

William Glasser's *Reality Therapy*, for which Mowrer wrote the preface, has made a significant impact upon contemporary psychotherapy. Certainly many will agree that his emphasis upon responsibility has provided a needed corrective to the ethical ambiguities of so-called "insight therapies." However, his assumptions regarding reality, responsibility, right and wrong, raise many questions of ultimate consequence which are critical to the whole approach.

Another serious theological critique of these points of view arises from assumptions regarding responsibility for guilt. This has to do with an implied "harshness" in their stress upon individual guilt and responsibility. Allowing for the realistic, hard-nosed, practical wisdom required in relating to delinquent individuals which Glasser ably and convincingly demonstrates, one runs the risk in generalizing from his data to an individual ethic.

His (and Mowrer's) implicit rejection of antinomian tendencies within society is healthy and needed. However, the logical extremes to which this points are legalism and the moralism which supports it. Helmut Thielicke asserts:

[4] Mowrer, *The Crisis in Psychiatry and Religion* (New York: D. Van Nostrand, 1961), p. 83.

The legal concept of guilt is . . . transcended by the spiritual concept in that the divine judgment is not only more radical but more merciful than the judgment of men. . . . The eternal Judge is at once both more severe and more compassionate; more severe in that he sees the whole of human powers at work in any particular sin an individual commits; and more compassionate in that he thus does not make this individual the sole guilty one, but always turns to the others, asking which of them dares to cast the first stone. (John 8:7.)[5]

Thus, "total guilt" is acknowledged as that arising from social and economic conditions which are partly the responsibility of the whole community. Certainly this is not to excuse the individual, but properly to broaden the base of responsibility. It is to accuse the "tongue cluckers" who may be in hearty agreement with Glasser as they condemn certain obvious forms of personal irresponsibility while they perpetuate and justify certain subtle forms of their own.

Total guilt lays upon the Christian "the obligation not merely to react to such cases from the point of view of 'individual ethics,' but rather by changing the conditions and eliminating the structural causes of such offenses by means of giving helpful assistance." [6]

In saying this I do not intend in any sense to minimize individual responsibility. On the contrary, my intent is to intensify it. I am arguing for a perspective upon the reality of total guilt and the assimilation of the judgment it carries, which includes the charge actively to support enlightened and responsible efforts to change the structures which breed and nourish personal irresponsibility. Of course, this

[5] Thielicke, *The Ethics of Sex* (New York: Harper & Row, 1964), p. 229.
[6] *Ibid.*, p. 230.

includes individual responsibility, which actually engenders radical structural changes. But we cannot, even by insisting that we are arguing strictly from a psychological perspective, leave the onus of responsibility on the individual. If this is not implied, then Mowrer and Glasser should say so. Mowrer's claim that the developing emphasis upon group therapy takes cognizance of the social dimensions of the issue at hand seems to me to be only a partial answer. Otherwise, we are left with no alternative except the Pelagian "hang-up" which I have already suggested.

The Nature of the Assimilation Process

Why is the assimilation of judgment necessary? Real change and transformation within a person or group depend upon it. A person may be unusually perceptive, with tremendous insight, sharply analytical, and quite articulate about his needs; but unless his insights, etc., become a part of him, they are wasted.

We have said judgment is the act of discerning, discriminating, and differentiating internal and external data. These data are received from the self, from others, and from God. They must be taken into the self if judgment is to contribute to the growth of the person. This "taking in" process is what we are calling assimilation.

The metaphor "assimilation" was borrowed from human nutrition because it describes a remarkably similar process to that of the organism's incorporation of food. The metaphor actually appears in the New Testament in another context:

For though by this time you ought to be teachers, you need some one to teach you again the first principles of God's word.

You need milk, not solid food; for every one who lives on milk is unskilled in the word of righteousness, for he is a child. *But solid food is for the mature, for those who have their faculties trained by practice to distinguish (pros diakrisin) good from evil.* (Heb. 5:12-14.)

In nutrition, assimilation means "the appropriation and incorporation of food into the appropriating body." Thus, in the physiological application it is the act of converting incorporated nutritive material into the fluid or solid substance of the body. It is the act of transforming into the body that which is new to the body.

Analogously, the assimilation of judgment is the process of taking into one's self judgments upon one's self—judgments from others and from God—and reworking them into one's self-concept, transforming the self-concept in accordance with insights thus derived, testing out the self-concept in actual situations, acting in a manner consistent with the revised concept, and opening one's self to further judgment. As judgments are assimilated, the capacity to take in judgment is increased.

Just as in human nutrition, wherein organic malfunctioning or the lack of nutritional elements inhibits the assimilation process with a deleterious effect on the whole body, avoidance of judgment or resistance to what judgment teaches impoverishes the whole personality. The assimilation of judgment adds dimensions of depth and breadth to the self and increases one's capacity for discernment.

Love at the Right Time

Can we say specifically what are the dynamics of the process of assimilation of judgment? Can we identify the power within interpersonal encounter which effects change and transformation within the persons involved? I think we can. Tillich's analysis of the forces at work within history is helpful at this point. He addresses himself to the fundamental question: What is a relevant ethic in a world about which one can say that the only sure characteristic is rapid change? He sees it as that implied on the basis of Christian ethics; namely, love dominated by *agape*. "*Love alone can transform itself according to the concrete demands of every individual and social situation without losing its eternity and dignity and unconditional validity.*" [7]

Tillich puts the answer to an ethical relativism which makes "change the ultimate principle" in terms of the union between love, *agape* and *kairos* (the right moment). He defines *kairos*, in his use of the term, as "the historical moment when something new, eternally important, manifests itself in temporal forms, in the potentialities and tasks of a special period." [8] Whatever the novelty is, it is distinctly appropriate and relevant to the existential situation. Appropriation of its meaning and significance, and the translation of that into new structures, has yet to take place, however. We have termed this the assimilation process. The organism, whether it be an institutional body or an individual, must revise itself *in detail* to turn the judgment ushered in by the new into forms which manifest it.

I see this applying to understanding phenomena encountered in pastoral counseling as well as to the analysis of moral action within history. Since the person certainly is not isolated from his world—the context of meaning and history within which he lives—he is affected by the same basic principles that are in operation in that world. This

[7] *Morality and Beyond*, p. 89.
[8] *Ibid.*

43

seems so obvious that it does not require belaboring. However, for purposes of emphasis, I submit that the principle I have affirmed pervades personal as well as historical events.

The union of love and *kairos* in the interpersonal process, we have implied throughout, is experienced by the person involved as judgment in some form. Such union is preliminary to the incorporation of judgment. His encounter of judgment as love "at the right time" enables him to take in the data which effect change and transformation in him. He may listen many times but not really hear what is being spoken to him. Now he hears. He hears because he is experiencing love at the right time.

A vivid illustration of the personal dimensions of the union of *agape* and *kairos* is seen in the following interview I had with a woman in her early forties. Her fictitious name is Evelyn Korr. She was a tall, lithe, blonde-haired woman, who was impeccably groomed and tastefully dressed. Her soft blue eyes portrayed a rather circumspect innocence.

She gave the initial appearance of being casual and aloof about what was going on around her. I was soon to discover that this manner was a facade, covering up considerable anxiety. She said she was "mildly concerned" about her husband who she felt might be having an "affair" with a younger woman. I was seeing her husband, who confirmed his wife's suspicion and was disgusted with her for not taking the matter seriously.

Mrs. Korr was withdrawn. She confessed that her range of interests was rather limited. Her activities were also circumscribed. I found I was continually forced to draw her out.

Mr. Colston: How do you feel about coming here?
Mrs. Korr: Better now. At first I didn't want to come. I

didn't know what I could say to you. (She gives an embarrassed laugh and gestures, indicating frustration.) I find that you are easy to talk to, so I am more relaxed about it. I knew I had to do something, so I figured I'd better come.

Mr. Colston: You say you "had to do something." Were you beginning to get alarmed about what was going on?

Mrs. Korr: Oh, I don't know. If she'd let him alone, I don't think there would be any problem.

Mr. Colston: You blame her for keeping after him.

Mrs. Korr: (She shakes her head affirmatively, looks at her hands for an interval and sits quietly. Finally, she looks up at me.) I can't believe he's really interested in her. I think it's just an affair. We've always got along . . . ah . . . I mean . . . sexually . . . and otherwise. I don't see any reason why he should be unhappy. Oh, we don't talk much, but we don't seem to have to.

Mr. Colston: So you really can't believe that you need to take Howard's friendliness for Betty very seriously?

Mrs. Korr: (She simply shakes her head. Her expression is pained, but she does not speak for several seconds.) I don't think so, but I don't know.

Mrs. Korr also stated that she had wished for some time she could talk with someone, but they disliked their minister so much that they could not go to him. Parenthetically again, Mr. Korr had complained that he was "hearing the minister run down too much." He went to church to worship, he declared, not to find fault with the preacher, and he felt guilty "for them" (the people doing the criticizing) and for even listening to it.

In the second interview she reiterated what she later confessed to me was her "whistling in the dark" theme. Her attitude in the early part of the session seemed to be one of general apathy. She presented a face of indifference, protesting—too much, it seemed to me—how unaffected she was by her husband's "affair." I sensed considerable anxiety behind what she was doing and saying and decided to tap it.

Mr. Colston: I hear you saying, now, that you are quite worried about the possibility of losing your husband.

Mrs. Korr: (She looks at me intently for a long moment. Tears are welling up in her eyes. She lowers her head.) Yes (weakly). Yes, it's true I'm really scared. (She breaks down and weeps. After several minutes she takes several tissues from the box on my desk and dries her eyes. She looks up at me again, and smiles weakly.) I'm sorry. I guess I needed to do that.

Mr. Colston: Yes, of course.

Mrs. Korr: (She looks at me imploringly.) What am I going to do?

Mr. Colston: You said before that you rarely talk to your husband. Maybe that's the place to begin, eh?

Mrs. Korr: I suppose . . . I have a lot of trouble telling him how I feel—but—ah—I guess I'll have to make myself do it.

As she rose to leave my office I could see the effects of the total impact of the session. Her shoulders were hunched. Her face was pale. She was obviously hurt, yet I could distinguish relief, too, in her strained countenance.

The following evening Mr. Korr came in for his scheduled appointment. He sat in the chair resolutely and looked me in the eye.

"What did you do to my wife last night?" he demanded abruptly and bluntly. I thought, "Oh, oh, here it comes!"

"She was rather shaken up, I know," I replied.

"Well, you must have said something to her. She didn't say what, but she came home and talked with me all night. Actually we were communicating better than any time in all the years of our marriage. I found myself feeling warm toward her—not pity which I often feel—but warmth. It's hard to explain what happened. Usually I get disgusted with her because she's always trying to cling to me. But I felt last night that I was getting some glimpses of the person in her. She said she wanted to read with me, discuss things, and understand more. I found the change hard to believe, but I must say it's encouraging."

When Mrs. Korr returned the following week, she was actually loquacious, whereas she had been almost uncommunicative. "This has been a good week," she began. "I have started to do some reading and to get involved in discussions. Why, do you know what I even did? I called our minister and asked him for an appointment for next Monday. I have decided to ask forgiveness for the rude way I have treated him. I still don't agree with him about a lot of things, but I don't have to be nasty about it. He seemed to welcome my coming."

We missed a full week of counseling after the third session. Upon my return, Mrs. Korr was the first to have an appointment with me. A few of the highlights of the interview are as follows:

Mrs. Korr: You know, I told you I had an appointment with our minister. Well, I went and I am glad I did. He was quite pleased that I had taken the trouble to come and see him. I let him know exactly how I felt about him. He didn't get angry like I thought he would. He said he knew I didn't like him, and he wasn't sure why, so he appreciated knowing how I felt. He said he hoped we could feel as free to talk with each other in the future as we were then. I said I hoped so, too. I went away feeling a lot better about him.

Mr. Colston: You are seeing him in a better light.

Mrs. Korr: Yes, I think so. (She sits silently for a moment. Then, with a heavy sigh, she continues.) How can people be so dense? I see people going around in a fog and I feel like shouting, "Hey, do what I did, wake up!" (She snaps her fingers.) I was blind, just sheer, stark blind! I didn't know what was going on in the world. Isn't that awful, to live more than forty years and not know what's going on? To think your own little private world is all there is? How could I be so stupid? I was looking, but I wasn't seeing. What's that scripture verse, "seeing they see not, and hearing, they hear not"? Well, that really says it. I've been seeing, but not seeing. It's just like coming out of a cave. Howard was right when he pointed out to me how we've been living in a narrow little groove. I can see it now, and I want to change it.

Mrs. Korr was describing quite well the emergence of "the new being," which Tillich has designated that which emerges from the union of *agape* and *kairos*.[9] She was seeing this phenomenon in her personal experience. Later she would begin to conceptualize her understanding of it, thus undertaking a later phase of the assimilation process.

The assimilation process occurs within a community, even if that community is only two persons. The significant other person is needed. In pastoral counseling, of course, this is the pastor. Although a person may have excellent insight into his own patterns and needs, he realizes he must communicate these to someone even to take his insights into himself. Behind this phase of his facing his existential situation is the necessity for exposing himself to the larger community to which he gives his loyalty. He forms and is transformed by that larger community.

[9] *Morality and Beyond*, p. 89.

Increasing the Capacity for Assimilation

Having achieved a new level of responsibility, the person finds he has opened himself to new occasions for judgment. His learning and growth depend upon assimilation of such judgments, and so on. Therefore, the process of assimilation, when it is performing its proper function, may be described as a continual movement from an externalizing to internalizing, back to an externalizing occupation with judgment, a process which goes on repeatedly throughout a person's life.

The person may remain, to a greater or lesser degree, unaffected by what he confronts in the various occasions and dimensions of judgment. Through such forfeiture, he loses even occasions for further judgment, which may immediately seem more comfortable and thus satisfying, but in the long run is likely to produce judgment of such consequence he cannot possibly assimilate it. The wisdom in the parable of the three servants seems applicable here:

Then the man who had been given one bag came and said, "Master, I knew you to be a hard man: you reap where you have not sown, you gather where you have not scattered; so I was afraid, and I went and hid your gold in the ground. Here it is—you have what belongs to you." "You lazy rascal!" said the master. "You knew that I reap where I have not sown, and gather where I have not scattered? Then you ought to have put my money on deposit, and on my return I should have got it back with interest. Take the bag of gold from him, and give it to the one with the ten bags. For the man who has will always be given more, till he has enough and to spare; and the man who has not will forfeit even what he has. Fling the useless servant out into the dark, the place of wailing and grinding of teeth!" (Matt. 25:24-30 NEB.)

Clearly this is a lesson on the nature of responsibility. It is in this sense that the parable applies to the assimilation of judgment. Through defensive action, hiding, covering up, "burying" the data one receives, or some other tactic of avoidance, one loses whatever capacity he possesses for the confrontation of judgment.

Description of the Stages

In the main, the process of the assimilation of judgment may be described as a reciprocal movement from externalization to internalization of judgments from all sources. As the person takes in what he experiences as judgment from outside himself, he internalizes it. This does not mean he has assimilated the judgment he has internalized. Only as he is able to sift out and refine judgments he brings into juxtaposition with his existing self-concept does he assimilate the judgment. Why depend on the terms "externalization" and "internalization" to convey what is meant here? Why not draw upon the generally applied concepts "objectivity" and "subjectivity"? The reason the former terms are preferred is that they seem to reflect the dynamic character of the process better than the more descriptive "objective" and "subjective."

I have observed seven stages in the internalizing-externalizing process: (1) *antithetical,* in which the person experiences judgment as alien, opposed, or "over against" him; (2) *interrogatory,* in which he begins inquiry into the specific meaning of the judgment he is experiencing for himself; (3) *conjunctive,* wherein he makes connections between the answers he brings to the questions he raises and his prevailing self-image; (4) *discriminative,* which marks the beginning of discernment as to what decisions occasioned by judgment are viable ones for him; (5) *con-solidative*, in which the person tests out his decisions in concrete situations and verifies his changing self-concept experimentally; (6) *dialectical*, or the stage wherein the person conceptualizes his understanding of his expanding self-consciousness; (7) *transformative*, the stage in which the person is conscious of change, and perhaps uses the past tense of verbs in describing his former self.[10]

The transition from one stage to another comes at a point of readiness and timeliness.[11] Furthermore, a subse-

[10] When I first became aware of "stages" in the process of the as-similation of judgment and began to reflect upon the dynamics of each of these stages, I was surprised that Greek terms persistently occurred to me as I endeavored to describe the process. Not being a scholar of the Greek language (having had only a few courses in New Testament Greek), I struggled with the English equivalents of the concepts with which I had been impressed in an effort to convey my understanding of the phenomena.

I submit the following outline of the stages as they originally came to me. A transliteration of the Greek word and a key English word stating its literal meaning are included:
Stage 1. antithetic: opposition
Stage 2. zetetic: inquiry
Stage 3. syndetic: binding together
Stage 4. dioristic: discrimination
Stage 5. docemastic: a testing
Stage 6. dialectic: a discourse
Stage 7. metamorphic: transformation
In some instances several English words are needed to give the shades of meanings which I perceived in the phenomena attendant to each stage.

[11] Jean Piaget has set forth a series of stages in his classic study of the development of moral judgment in children, *The Moral Judgment of the Child* (Glencoe, Ill.: The Free Press, 1948), pp. 13-19. From his ob-servation of children learning "the rules of the game of marbles," Piaget discerned that children follow a logical sequence in their development of "consciousness of the rules." By questioning the children, or, as he called it, "carrying on an interrogatory," he was able to distinguish four stages in the child's assimilation of the meaning of the rules:

The first stage is a *motor* or individual stage in which the child experiences the strangeness of the marbles, but begins to handle them and to become familiar with their "feel." He forms "ritualized schemes" for play.

quent stage apparently emerges from a previous whole pattern of organization. Consequently, the person has to work through each stage, become aware of what he is learning, and integrate the data into his self-understanding and functioning.

When one acknowledges that a particular pattern of behavior is harmful, baneful, or just pointless and fruitless, he has become aware of implicit or explicit judgment from some source. He may resolve to change his behavior and set out to do so. Or he may simply seek reassurance, reinforcement of his own feelings, pity, or a combination of these. In any case, he is unquestionably motivated by his own anxiety and resulting tension to try a different approach. In many instances, a person experiences temporary relief from symptoms and does nothing further. Consequently, judgment is not assimilated.

Ultimately, then, discipline is the key to the assimilation of judgment. "Working through" the stages requires patient, persistent effort. It means bearing a little pain now for the sake of greater health in the long run. "It is for discipline that you have to endure," says the author of Hebrews. "God is treating you as sons; for what son is there

---

The second stage is *egocentric*, combining imitation of others with purely individual use of what he has learned.

The third stage is called incipient *cooperation*, wherein there is some meeting of understanding regarding rules, but a lack of unanimity in interpreting them.

Finally, the fourth stage is *codification* of rules, or a more discriminating understanding and application of rules within the whole society.

There are apparent similarities between the scheme I have devised and that of Piaget, but there was no conscious modeling after his. The fact that we perceived stages of a process independently would seem to argue for the validity of both schemes. Piaget noted that the developing moral discrimination of the child passed through stages roughly equivalent to age levels, whereas I am showing stages in their accelerated and more complex form in adults.

whom his father does not discipline? If you are left without discipline, in which all have participated, then you are illegitimate children and not sons. . . . For the moment all discipline seems painful rather than pleasant; later it yields the peaceful fruit of righteousness to those who have been trained by it." (Heb. 12:7-8, 11.)

The goal of the Christian life, according to the apostle Paul, for instance, is change and transformation. The change is in the direction of a transformed image. "Just as we have borne the image of the man of dust, we shall also bear the image of the man of heaven," he exhorted the Corinthians in a discussion of resurrection. (I Cor. 15:49.) This was not purely a reference to an event at some time in the future, but also a present reality of which Paul was immediately aware. He was witnessing to his existential experiencing of "passing from death into life," a reality which justified his faith.

The assimilation of judgment is required for personal growth. The process occurs under the conditions of love and *kairos*. Each gain increases one's capacity for further assimilation and intensifies his sense of responsibility. The assimilation process consists of seven characteristic stages, each of which is regarded as essential to change and transformation in the person. In the following chapters we will further define each stage and illustrate it with case material.

PART II

4 The Enemy Without and Within

When a person becomes aware of judgment, he usually experiences it as pure threat. Whether positive or negative, judgment is perceived as alien, perhaps even as undeserved. At any rate, judgment is usually first seen cloaked as the enemy. Initially, the data of the judgment are not trusted, even if the truth in them is faintly recognized. Yet acknowledgment of the enemy-judgment is a hopeful sign, because it signals the promise of creative conflict without which personal growth is hardly possible. Ignoring judgment throws one into the often frenetic "rear trench" operations of building defenses while being cheated of the ultimate prize—personal discipline and enhancement.

This first stage in the assimilation of judgment is called *antithetical*, because the term best describes the relationship the person feels to the judgment of which he is aware. The judgment in some sense contradicts the person's view of himself. He sees the judgment as opposition—as strange to him.

Drawing upon Piaget's insight into the first stage of the child's moral discernment, we may say: now that the person acknowledges judgment as bearing some relationship to him, he must handle it to get the feel of it. In the interpersonal process, the indication is toward considerable wrestling with the judgment in the encounter with the other to test his power in relation to it.

A certain primordial experiencing of this phenomenon is revealed in the Genesis account of Jacob's wrestling with God and the ultimate judgment of God upon Israel, which is symbolized in the narrative. It is thus in the initial phase of any creative relationship. As one vies with the strength of the other in the encounter, his own real strength is brought out. As the Jacob narrative has it—both are blessed! (Gen. 32:24-32.)

Reactions to the Enemy

In the antithetical stage, the person's usual reaction to judgment (which we have said is perceived as threat, but may also be promise) is self-pitying or self-justifying (defensive). He has become aware of judgment, and, if he is seeking pastoral counseling, he is motivated to do something about it, even if it means only angling for the pastor's support of his resistance to what the judgment is about. Usually, however, the person is earnestly seeking to understand how he is being judged, as indeed he is, and what he can effectively do about it.

However, his perception of the judgment of which he is aware is often undifferentiated (generalized, not specific in detailed knowledge), undiscerning (vague and ambiguous), and undiscriminating (confused, not sharp as to what is distinctive). For example, the person may see judgments as threats whether they are constructive in intent or not.

If a person or a group is in a state of rebellion against another person or group or against God, they often are undiscriminating in their judgment, even while they are sharply aware of who the enemy is. Thus, this person or group tends categorically to reject the good along with the bad and to obscure both the positive and negative aspects of the judgment they receive.

Discriminative encounter with judgment begins as one acknowledges and accepts the antithetical character of judgment—whether it is positive or negative—and courageously confronts the opposition it represents to him. The requirement indicated here may be paraphrased in the aphorism attributed to St. Francis: "The courage to change what can be changed, the faith to accept what cannot be changed, and the *wisdom to know the difference*" (italics mine). The latter is underscored to give emphasis to our argument and to depict the goal of the process.

This is not to equate judgment with wisdom, but to state what is crucial—namely, through continual encounter with judgment one may become more discerning as to what he may learn from it. The "over-againstness" provides sharp contrast and differentiation. If it is in the context of love, judgment thus calls one into a responsible and creative relationship. By the same token, negatively speaking, avoidance of encounter with judgment and rejection of its antithetical character obviously prevent one from assimilating judgment, and lead him to blur the distinction between what he is and what he may become.

An illustration of a negative response to judgment is given in the following account of a Korean War veteran's struggle with the concept of God's forgiveness.[1] He has consulted the pastor about his deep doubts regarding what he had been taught previously and how he had come into conflict with that teaching. The actual interview is as follows:

[1] Newman S. Cryer, Jr., and John M. Vayhinger, *Casebook in Pastoral Counseling* (Nashville: Abingdon Press, 1962), pp. 267-70.

John: Afternoon, Reverend L.

Pastor: Hi, John! How are you today?

John: Not so good. I called you earlier in the week. I thought I ought to come down and talk to you for a while.

Pastor: Uh-huh.

John: I don't know exactly what it is, but I haven't been feeling too well.

Pastor: Something's been bothering you?

John: Well, it's pretty mixed up. Not only home and office, it's all over. I think I know pretty much what it is, but I can't seem to figure it out.

Pastor: Things seem rather confusing? You almost think you know, but you're not quite sure?

John: Yes. (*Pause.*) Reverend, can God forgive people?

Pastor: I think he can. What do you think about it?

John: I don't know. I thought so too, but that was before. Now I don't know—I don't know.

Pastor: You have some doubts about the forgiving nature of God?

John: Yeah—maybe I better tell you. It was five years ago. I've never told anybody this. It's been bothering me so much I just had to tell somebody: I killed five men. It was during the Korean War. I just got married and was drafted and went overseas right away. One night when we were out on patrol, three of us and the lieutenant went out on a mission. I was the only one who came back. We started out and everything was okay. We got there and took care of our mission and on the way back it happened—we were ambushed. I sort of got cut off from the others. I heard shots. I laid in the grass. They went on by; then I found myself behind the lines and couldn't get back. I wasn't too sure where I was so I just started crawling. Then I saw them: three pillboxes on one side and a river on the other. The only way I could get them was one at a time. So I did. Crawled up—Couldn't shoot—too many—pulled out my knife, bayonet, got all five, one at a time. Didn't bother me at first, even when I came back from the war. Didn't bother too much. But then I got to thinking about it. All the time God says, "Thou shalt not kill." But I did. I killed—five of them—stuck a knife right through each one.

Pastor: This has caused you some amount of worry since you have come back?

John: Yeah. You know how I've been with the church. I started sort of worrying more and more all the time. God is supposed to be able to forgive people, but this is sort of different. This isn't the same thing as when you preach up there on Sunday morning. You sort of get up and tell about these people. The little things—cheating at business, a heavy finger on the scale, or something like that—but this is different. This is a big business; this is murder.

Pastor: The experience in the army is a very big thing to you in relation to some of the things we preach about?

John: Not so much the experience, but the killing. I just killed these men. I know, it might have been them or me. Maybe it would have been better if it had been me. I don't know. I've just been waiting, waiting for something to happen. I don't think God can just come out and forgive this kind of thing. I don't know. Just seems—I don't know.

Pastor: Things have been building up inside of you, and you have begun to question God's activity in this?

John: Yeah, I guess, sort of. Well, God—he's running the universe you might say. You just can't go around killing people right and left without being punished for it. God just doesn't sit there and let you stab people and let you get away with it. In our society, just like a man kills somebody, we kill him sometimes. This is almost the same thing. I mean, you take a life. You just don't go out and do this. You say, "Well, it's over with, it's part of the war"; but it's more than that. It's a man you killed. Just like if I killed somebody now, it's the same thing.

61

Pastor: Then you are wondering now how God can forgive one who has killed?

John: Yeah, that's about it. I don't know. I've been waiting; I've been hoping; I've even been praying. But I don't think he's forgiven me. He—I just keep worrying. Now I think I'm going to get punished; I don't know. I know he's going to punish me somehow. I don't know how. But I think this is it; this is what's bothering me. I just keep waiting, looking every day. I wake up and I look out and I think well, maybe today he'll punish me so I can go on living like I should. But he hasn't punished me. He just keeps me waiting.

Pastor: Waiting for punishment is a terrible threat.

This young veteran has a concept of God as rigid and judgmental. He undoubtedly has it all mixed up with previous experiences of parental authority. At any rate, he has not yet been able to distinguish between God's judgment and his forgiveness, hence his own guilt has become unbearable to him. God's judgment is definitely seen as opposition. Whether or not he is able to work through this stage depends in large part on whether the pastor can do more than help him to acknowledge the guilt. The pastor must face the issue and deal with the guilt along *with* the young man.

Paul E. Johnson, commenting on this case, raises the pertinent questions:

Can the pastor honestly take a holier-than-thou attitude, or permit the war guilt to fall on this one guilt-laden man to bear alone his staggering burden?

Is not society guilty, too, and is not the pastor, together with the writer and reader of this page, involved and accountable with church and nation for neglecting a better way than mass murder, which has settled little but to make a solution more difficult?

The counselor might prefer to avoid judgment, yet he knows that all stand under God's judgment.[2]

The pastor, in this interview, has done little actually to communicate to the young veteran that he is truly *with* him. He fails to establish the common bond of humanity— the meeting ground upon which a genuine encounter between them can take place. If the pastor is to represent God here, then he must *show* how God accepts man's doubts and reaches through them to embrace man. To reveal that he neither feels nor understands his own implicit involvement in the guilt the young man is facing is for the pastor to find himself under judgment.

The point is: the pastor must guard against subtly or openly reinforcing the person's experiencing of judgment as opposition. The pastor, after all, is also human. He may have his own problems with judgment. However, as pastor he is presumably witnessing to the constructive character of God's judgment in the world. He fails if he continually underscores the antithetical stage of judgment. He is helpful as he supports the assimilation process. He does so in loving encounter of the other in the humble recognition that all, including himself, fall short and stand under God's judgment.

Judgment as opposition is the "kairos opportunity" for the person who is being confronted in that his acknowledgment signals his readiness for the encounter from which he now realizes he cannot emerge unchanged. The person indicates his willingness to take the risk of confrontation. Judgment presents that opportunity to him. He may accept it and face the prospect of suffering, but also the possibility of creative change in himself.

[2] *Ibid.*, p. 272.

The following excerpt from a significant interchange among several members of a group illustrates this point. A minister was the group leader. Members of the group had been associated for a short period of time. They were just beginning to experience freedom in their group relationships. The group consisted of laymen who, along with their minister, had decided to form their own "sensitivity group."

In this particular interaction, Mr. Bode, a thirty-five-year-old businessman was expressing his feelings to Mr. Camm, a forty-year-old professional man.

Mr. Bode: Why is it that ministers are always on the wrong side of issues today? I don't think most of these guys know what people are thinking. Many of them seem to be afraid to say anything. They give the impression they are always apologizing for who and what they are. This bothers me. I wish they had the guts to stand up and be counted.

The Minister: Hey, you are pretty hostile to ministers, aren't you?

Mr. Camm: (interrupting) Look, Jim, a lot of ministers are taking courageous stands today. You are generalizing all over the place. And, anyway, why are you always attacking Joe (the minister)?

Mr. Bode: What I want to know is: why are you always defending him? Is it important to you to be on "daddy's" side all the time?

Mr. Camm: It seems to me you are trying to be the analyst of the group. Why don't you just come on in and be one of us?

Mr. Bode: Well, I will say I have been pretty threatened by you, Bill. I have a lot of respect for you because I think you are well informed. But I made up my mind to get you involved too and not let you be another leader of the group, while "Mr. Nice Guy" (he tosses his head in the direction of the minister) sits over there and lets you do it.

The Minister: So, you regard me as trying to protect a "nice guy" image and you doubt that I can effectively challenge any effort on Bill's part to take over.

Mr. Bode: Well, I'd like to think you would. I don't know. Bill's a sharp operator.

Mr. Camm: No. I just get annoyed with you because I think you are trying to take over the leader's role in the group. I don't see you as succeeding although I think you'd like to.

Mr. Bode: You've got me all wrong.

Mr. Camm: Have I?

Mr. Bode: Yes. I have the greatest respect for Joe. I don't think I could even talk like this in this group if I didn't. I admit I am probably baiting Joe to get some answers to some of these questions about his profession that have been bugging me, but I am somehow not trying to take over his leadership. In fact, I have been thinking all along that I was helping him. Obviously, you see my motives differently.

Mr. Camm: I do and I think most of the other members of the group do, if I am able to size up their reactions, but they should speak for themselves.

(Mr. Bode looks intently at Mr. Camm for a strained moment, then speaks.)

Mr. Bode: O.K. I admit I have had some ideas about how this group should be run. When it comes right down to it, though, I think you are as much of a ——— as you seem to think I am.

(Mr. Camm laughs. They both laugh, and other members of the group laugh with them.)

Obviously, both Mr. Bode and Mr. Camm see the other as playing the game of replace the leader. Mr. Bode sees Mr. Camm as a smooth operator who is trying subtly to usurp the minister's leadership by giving the appearance of lining up with him. Mr. Camm, on the other hand, regards Mr. Bode as an aggressive aspirant to leadership of the group. Each is seeking to expose what he regards as the real motives of the other.

At this point the implicit judgment in the encounter is antithetical to both Mr. Bode and Mr. Camm. However, they meet on the ground of their common humanity and the recognition that ultimately both are judged. This awareness on their part and on the part of the whole group temporarily breaks the tension and sets up the moratorium during which they will assimilate the judgment they have experienced.

The first stage in the assimilation of judgment is called *antithetical*. The term describes the person's awareness of judgment as over against him. Recognition of the contrast between judgments he holds and judgments he receives opens up creative possibilities to the person. If he does not acknowledge the distinct opposition of these judgments, he runs the risk of eliminating sharp contrasts from his whole life and seeks to avoid the difficult task of assimilating judgment. Ultimately the enemy judgment must be recognized as true friend and embraced as such.

5 What Is Required?

The second stage is interrogation. Once the person acknowledges judgment as opposition, he desires to know the "whys" and "hows." Thus begins a period of scrutiny, inquiry, analysis, examination, and investigation of specific judgments to determine their particular meanings for the person. He questions the judgments of others about him and analyzes his self-judgments to bring them into sharper focus in an effort to correct whatever distortions are in them.

Inquiry is thus the chief mode of confronting judgment in the interrogatory stage. By raising questions within himself and with others, he seeks to get a perspective upon the data of the judgment of which he is now aware. He wishes to clarify his understanding of what he is experiencing. Is the judgment relevant? Is it accurate? Does it primarily reflect the biases of the judging one? Can I trust it? What must I do about it? Are the judgments, whether seen as coming from God or other persons, really just and fair? These are some of the types of questions which arise during the interrogatory stage.

Inquiry is the act of entering into relationship with a person, a body of knowledge, or a datum. Interest in a person, for example, cues off a series of questions by which one seeks to gain knowledge about the person. Of course, if the other does not wish to be known (at least he may not wish to reveal himself to the questioner because he does not trust him), he will turn off the questions or be evasive in his answers. Inquiry in a relationship, therefore, is in itself a judgment. In its wholehearted sense it means: "I regard you as worth knowing and therefore I invite you to reveal yourself to me." Of course, if this approach is sincere, it will be accompanied by a spirit of mutuality, in which the interrogator is as willing to reveal himself as he is to ask the other to do so. Inquiry may not be wholehearted, in which case it arises from the motive of using data thus obtained to one's own advantage and possibly to the hurt of the other.

Analogously, inquiry regarding the data of judgment is a way of becoming familiar with judgment and making it a part of one, just as a person thus encountered may become an integral part of the other. To carry the analogy further: judgment is not disembodied. Every person one truly meets becomes a judgment in some form upon him. He either has to live up to or live down the judgments in terms of which he is perceived by others. Judgment is embodied in concrete persons, and a person faces it every time he meets another.

Inquiry is the first step toward differentiation of the data of judgment coming from all sources. Specific questions break into these data at given points, enabling the person to bring the data into relationship with his present self-understanding. We are reminded again that a wholesale rejection of the data of judgment out of fear of their threatening character prevents a person from entering into the stage of inquiry. If he doesn't raise questions, he is not forced to deal with troublesome answers. He gives up his true heritage by sacrificing freedom for what he believes is security.

An example of the struggle typical of the second stage is seen in the following portion of an early interview with Mr. Kronn, a forty-year-old government employee.

Mr. Kronn: I don't know what's right. I think it actually makes me a little angry—ah—I simply don't know. I don't think I ever have. I don't think I ever knew what I was— ah—what I was supposed to do in college. I never did. I never knew at all—or clearly—for fifteen years, what it was really all about. So I never felt I had any calling or purpose or goal, but I always said a person ought to have. I've wondered if other people were doing better in this regard than me—except doctors and scientists.

Pastor: You are quite angry that you have not been able to see clearly where you are going, and, I gather, you wonder if other people have the same difficulty.

Mr. Kronn: Yeah. (He pauses.) It bothers me, I feel—to be honest—I'm "moth-eatenly" so—but I'm fundamentally a religious person and I feel I've kind of goofed. I mean, ah —I feel that I've been sort of buried in the ground—and this troubles me very much—because I do feel that one is accountable for what he is given, and, ah—I've squandered mine. Oh, not in riotous living, darn it (he laughs)—just in *no* living, I guess you'd say. I feel that God is lawful— and I wonder, is it too late to do something now? Have I reached the point of no return?

Pastor: You fear that you have passed up all your opportunities—and—ah, that maybe your present torment is in some sense a judgment of God on you?

Mr. Kronn: Sure. (He strikes his fist on his thigh). But the only thing I can say is I couldn't have taken hold any earlier because I didn't know what I was supposed to do!

Pastor: So frustrating not to know what to do!

Mr. Kronn: Exactly. (He pauses as he sits back in his chair.) Like some people say—the trouble with me is that I'm in a hurry, and God is not. Now if you can take that view, it's fine. If I were satisfied to relax and say, well, like old Charlie does—Charlie says every place you go, that's the place you're supposed to be. I wonder if he's right? The only thing I can say is I'm like Moses in the desert. He took forty years to wander around. I guess he was just waiting for all the old "moss-backs" to die off, so he could do something for his people. (He laughs.) But—ah—

Pastor: (He laughs.) You see the strategy in his "sojourn in the desert," and—

Mr. Kronn: Yeah (he laughs), he was not so dumb—

Pastor: But, I guess, you wonder whether you are even now being rather impatient—

Mr. Kronn: Yeh, maybe so—maybe so. (He pauses.) Well, Father Squawk (the name he used to disguise the identity of the clergyman to whom he was referring) said—he was talking about himself—he said, "You know, I look back to see how I got where I am now and you know, I could not have done it any sooner." I've thought about that the last few days. Do you suppose that's part of the big trouble with me?

Pastor: I don't know. I guess as you reflect on your own behavior, you see that you have been rather ambitious and impatient with yourself for not getting there.

Mr. Kronn: Well, I guess my impatience has been with God, too, for not showing me the way, if I may be so bold as to say so! And—ah—if this is what he does—I don't know. This is what I'm wondering about. Is it just "thick me" or is he judging me this way?

The interview continued in this vein for the remainder of the hour, with Mr. Kronn raising repeated questions about his understanding of what he had been experiencing.

What did it mean? Where was he deficient? Or obtuse? Or just plain "cussed," as he put it at one point? Is God really just or primarily capricious? What was the specific nature of his (Mr. Kronn's) own guilt? As he carried on this "interrogatory" with himself and the pastoral counselor, he discussed each question as he saw it applying to him and examined its implications for his own self-concept. At the end of the counseling hour, as he rose to leave, Mr. Kronn remarked, jokingly, "Well—I didn't get many answers, but I sure raised lots of questions, didn't I?" Then he became quite serious again as if being careful to reassure the counselor of his good will, "No, but—this has been very helpful—it's given me a chance to get some things out and look at them—ah—I'll have quite a bit to think about before I see you next week."

Mr. Kronn was dealing with his own severe judgment of himself for his longtime pattern of squandering time. He interpreted the judgment he felt as God's judgment. He was disgusted with himself for thinking he could get away with "frittering." He really knew that he could not have his time strictly on his own terms. During this interrogatory stage, he hesitatingly but clearly blamed God for "not showing him the way." By strong implication this complaint was also leveled at the pastor. Obviously, impatience was precisely the term to describe Mr. Kronn's feeling toward the pastor, who was largely responding by reflecting what Mr. Kronn was communicating. Mr. Kronn desired a brisk engagement with the pastor; thus, in part, he was expressing his frustration with the counseling relationship.

His primary mode of relating at this juncture was that of inquiry. He sought to differentiate between what he was experiencing as a breakthrough of his own authority and what had been taught regarding authority, including the authority of God. He was mildly shocked at his own presumptuousness in daring to question external authorities; nevertheless, he could affirm this right without crippling fears of retaliation. Thus, he was beginning to try on his right to even question and was enjoying the freedom to do so.

Inquiry gives expression to the affective response to the experiencing of opposition in judgment and enables the person to become discerning of the specific data in that judgment. Just as a person desires to know what his opponent in any game or contest is really like, so that he may have some notion of what to expect, so also does one wish to know what is the nature of the judgment of which he is aware.

This was dramatically illustrated in a marriage counseling relationship with a middle-aged couple. Although they had been married for more than fifteen years, both felt they had never really communicated with each other. The woman, who was employed in industry as a highly trained professional, stated she was not sure she ever really loved her husband, but actually was overpowered by his aggressiveness in courting her. "I was weak," she groaned, "and just gave in to him, not realizing that was going to be the pattern of our married life."

The following occurred at the beginning of the sixth interview with the couple:

Mr. Bamm: Well, yesterday she filed for a divorce. I don't want it. I want her. She says she doesn't love me, but I don't believe this. Why, we've been married fifteen years. (He draws this out with strong feeling.) People don't stay married that long if there isn't something there. I don't understand her attitude. I've been a responsible husband and father all along. What am I doing that's wrong? (He directs this question to her.)

Mrs. Bamm: (She gestures rather resignedly and speaks softly.) It's not that you do anything. Oh, I don't know how to explain my feelings. I'm sorry, there just isn't anything there. I just don't seem to be able to say anything without his twisting it all around (she is looking directly at the pastor as she says this). He is so hard on our daughter (fourteen years of age)—makes her feel about this high (she raises two fingers indicating a small space between them).

Mr. Bamm: Well, somebody's got to discipline the girl! You don't! (He says this to her defiantly.) I think you'd just let her run wild. (He glares at her. She lowers her head and sits quietly. She bites her lip and fights to repress her tears.)

Minister: You despise her for being what you regard as too permissive with your daughter?

Mr. Bamm: Well, wouldn't you want to know where your daughter is at all times—especially with all that's going on in our city streets?

Minister: You mean you are justified in feeling the way you do?

Mr. Bamm: (He reacts disgustedly.) You are just like my wife —you keep trying to put it back on me. (He pauses, then he looks sharply at the minister.) I wish you would tell me what she really expects of me. (He looks at his wife.) Why don't you tell me specifically how I can change to please you? (She gestures hopelessly.) You see? (He speaks to the minister.) It's so frustrating! She won't even tell me what she doesn't like about me.

Minister: Did you hear what your wife said to you a while ago?

Mr. Bamm: I thought I did. Why? What have you got in mind?

Minister: That she wants only to be treated like a person.

Mr. Bamm: What the hell does that mean? That's sure vague!

Mrs. Bamm: I just don't dare open my mouth, because what I say gets twisted. I feel like I am in a law court most of the time.

Mr. Bamm: So you can't tell a story, and I have to jump in and straighten it out!

Mrs. Bamm: Well, I can't. You do a much better job of story-telling than I do. (She adds quickly.) That's only part of it.

Minister: I hear your wife saying she can't win with you, in fact she can't even compete. You can out-argue her. She feels overpowered and uncomfortable with you. I hear her saying also it is not what you *do* that bothers her, it's your attitude toward her. She is tired of being continually squelched.

Mr. Bamm: Then why doesn't she fight back instead of just taking it from me. . . . Do you think it will help our marriage if I try to change this?

Minister: I don't know. Apparently you feel that it may.

Mr. Bamm: (He arches his eyebrows and hunches his shoulders.) Well, it's worth a try.

Once Mr. Bamm could acknowledge the reality of the judgment he was confronting in his relationships with other people, he was motivated to try to understand it. His inquiry began within the whole patterned character of his self-concept. Thus his first questions grew out of the basic intention to prove the rightness of his thinking. Shortly, however, he was genuinely struggling to understand what could be done to win the affection of his wife. He was recognizing that his attitude toward her was a reproach to her for refusing him her love, but he felt caught in it. Mrs. Bamm interpreted his change of attitude as a prudential repentance which she could not trust.

74

Mrs. Bamm: Like the minister says, I'm tired of even trying to fight. You are more clever with words and arguments than I am, and you know it. So what are we trying to prove, that you are always right? I just can't live with this kind of tension all the time.

Mr. Bamm: Of course I am not always right—that's absurd! But I am trying to be responsible. I am not a rounder. I don't drink and carouse around.

Mrs. Bamm: Yes, you are "Mr. *Pure* and Right."

Minister: You resent what you see as his self-righteousness?

Mrs. Bamm: I don't resent him. I just don't have any feeling for him.

Minister: You put considerable feeling into that last retort to him. (She laughs and sits back in her chair. She looks at the minister intently.)

Mrs. Bamm: I don't hate him. I just don't have any feelings for him one way or the other. This bothers me, because I don't see it as really fair to him. I hate to hurt him, but I have to be honest with everybody concerned. I'd rather get a divorce than to go on being hypocritical.

Minister: You mean you regard your action as actually doing him a favor—ah—taking you off his hands, so to speak?

Mrs. Bamm: Maybe it does sound that way. But, I will admit, too, that he makes me awfully nervous. (She pauses.) I'm talking too much. I'll get the devil on the way home.

Mr. Bamm: You make me sound like an old ogre!

Mrs. Bamm: (She responds quickly, almost matter-of-factly.) Sometimes you *do* sound like one.

This exchange rather aptly characterizes the antithetical stage of judgment. I include this to give a brief background for what follows. The next interview, a week later, began rather slowly. Both were guarded in what they said.

The interrogatory stage was reached during this interchange.

Mr. Bamm: Why can't you tell me specifically what I can do differently? You know—one, two, three! I love this girl and I want to keep her. I want some answers! (He bangs the chair with his fist.)

Minister: You're going to wrench them out of me, is that it? You demand that I give you something? You are going to take me by force?

Mr. Bamm: (He slumps down in his chair.) OK . . . OK. So I am being impatient. You are right, this is what I do to my wife.

Minister: I hear you mention frequently the word "right." Is this of critical importance to you?

Mr. Bamm: I guess so. This is what my wife says, anyway.

Minister: But you don't see yourself that way?

Mr. Bamm: Well I do, but I don't see what's to change. I can't, or should I say won't, give up my basic principles. But what can I do to change, if that's what she wants?

Minister: Is it what you want?

Mr. Bamm: If there's a chance of keeping her, yes. But what should I do?

Minister: What do you think needs changing?

Mr. Bamm: I don't know. The obvious thing I can think of— and she reminds me of this once in a while—is that I jump on her to correct her in social situations. But it's hard for me to sit by and watch her mess something up.

Minister: It's hard for you to "sit by" and watch anybody "mess something up," isn't it?

Mr. Bamm: You make me sound like a tyrant. Is that the way I come through to you?

Minister: At times, yes.

Inquiry is the method of setting the intellectual process into motion. It is at the leading edge of learning experience. One can get bogged down here, just as he can in the antithetical stage, by using inquiry defensively. As in the case of Mr. Bamm, a person may be so preoccupied with establishing the "rightness" of his thinking that he is not open to the other person. However, inquiry serves the positive function of breaking into judgment for the purpose of comprehending it and seeking its particular relevance for the judged one.

The interrogatory stage is one in which *inquiry* is the primary method of dealing with judgment. The person seeks to know the nature of the judgment and its specific relevance to him. He questions how the judgment can give him a perspective upon himself and his situation. He is seeking to differentiate what the judgment is about. This is the phase of his counseling relationship which is marked by his struggle for understanding. If he can *see* what is required, he reasons, he may be enabled effectively to act wisely.

6   Binding the Data Together

"I really hadn't seen what I was doing," Mrs. Drann said, "but I was treating you the very same way I treat my husband. When you suggested something to me, I immediately got on the defensive. It's taking a lot of 'putting things together' to see exactly how and when I do this, but I am beginning to sift it out. Now when I begin to react, I sort of laugh inside because I know what I am doing and it strikes me as funny to see myself starting to do it. You know, understanding this is helping my relationship with my husband."

Mrs. Drann is describing the third stage in the process of the assimilation of judgment. I have labeled it the *conjunctive* stage, because the term best connotes the specific dynamics of that stage. It is the point at which considerable coordinating, bringing together, and relating the data of judgment which come from the various sources—self, others, and God—occurs. The person acts as his own "computer." In fact, the computer is really an extension of this internal process.

The conjunctive stage marks the first move toward a consolidation of gains in self-understanding, which have come from the previous stage of inquiry into the character of the judgment one perceives and feels. This stage is characterized chiefly by the action of bringing together what one learns from the judgment he confronts with his existing self-concept and the uniting of his judgments with his feelings.

Thus the term "consolidation" is also appropriate to indicate the activity typical of the conjunctive stage. The process is one of enlarging and strengthening the ego through bringing together experiences and feelings. Carl Rogers has termed the goal of such efforts "congruence." "Congruence is the term we have used to indicate an accurate matching of experiencing and awareness," Rogers asserts. "It may be still further extended to cover a matching of experience, awareness, and communication." [1] He illustrates with a reminder that a person can usually sense when the other is putting up a front or a facade and not communicating what he feels. The usual reaction to the person who presents such a front is to be wary and cautious of him. Consequently, the relationship is on very shaky grounds.

Once the person becomes more discerning of the judgments of the other, and receives them for what they are, rather than defending against them indiscriminately, he begins to come out from behind the facade. Or, to put it within the framework of the stage we are describing, he is able to bring together the data of the judgment with his feelings.

An example of the conjunctive stage in operation may be seen in the following pastoral counseling interview with Mr. Gaal, a thirty-five-year-old salesman. Mr. Gaal had been married for ten years. He and his wife had no children. He had persistently refused, saying he was not a

[1] *On Becoming a Person* (Cambridge: Riverside Press, 1961), p. 339.

"fit candidate for fatherhood." He had what he described as an "uncontrollable temper." "I am afraid to have a child," he said. "There are times when I just lose control, and I don't know what I'd do."

One evening the pastor received a telephone call from Mr. Gaal, who excitedly demanded to see the pastor immediately. The pastor was preparing to leave for the airport to catch a plane for a one-day trip to another city for a conference. He informed Mr. Gaal of his plans and offered to see him on the day of his return. Calming considerably, Mr. Gaal related to the pastor how that very afternoon he had "taken a swing" at one of the sales managers and had to be restrained by his colleague. "It's getting embarrassing. I'm afraid I am out at Perry Sales now. I seem to be letting go now more than I did, and it scares me. I don't know what I'm going to do. Sure, I want to see you as soon as I can when you get back."

During the initial interview Mr. Gaal first expressed surprise that he had not been "given the ax" by his employer, then went on to talk about his inability to control his temper. He explained he was not only hazarding his work, but also alienating his wife, who, he said, had been able to "tolerate" him up to now, but was getting extremely resentful of his refusal to have children. "But, I ask you, what kind of a father would I be?" he blurted, gesturing dramatically. He further expressed his alarm at his own impulsive behavior but protested his inability to do anything to change it. He pressed the pastor for an interpretation of his "problem" and for an immediate solution. When the pastor responded to Mr. Gaal's aggressive dependent attitude, Mr. Gaal became angry and remarked, "I never did like smug preachers."

On the day following the interview the pastor received

an apologetic call from Mr. Gaal with a request for another
appointment.

The significant point of that session was near the end of
the hour when the exchange was as follows:

Mr. Gaal: You know what came back to me this week. It
sounds so simple—ah—I wonder why I haven't thought of it
before—but, well—God! It just hit me! There was this man-
ual arts teacher I had in high school—for some reason he
didn't like me. I got picked on a lot when I was a kid—ah—
I was awkward—about as clumsy as they come. (He laughs.)
This guy—well, he joined in when the other guys razzed me.
I didn't take my own part much—ah—in fact I guess that's
part of why I got picked on—I just took it, see? Well, this
teacher flunked me. That's the only course I ever really
flunked. Boy, I hated his guts! But I never did say anything
to him—or—ah—to anybody for that matter. My dad gave me
the devil for flunking the course—and—ah—I never even told
him. Ah—the reason I am telling you this is: I don't think I
have ever got that thing out of my system. God! Anybody
starts razzing me—I see red! I got to thinking this week,
I've been taking it out on the wrong people ever since.

Pastor: I guess you're seeing that you have probably never
really dealt with that situation, and—

Mr. Gaal: Yeah, but that's not all! Ah—well, like the other
day—I went to this sales manager I was telling you about
and told him I was sorry about what happened, that I had
been pretty touchy lately. He said he didn't hold it against
me, to forget it and be friends, that I was a good man and
he didn't want to lose me from the force—he hadn't meant
to push me either. I can't remember ever doing anything
like that before—ah—I mean—trying to be friends with
somebody I thought needed a punch in the nose. (He
laughs.)

81

Pastor: This is a new feeling for you. You enjoy it—you respect yourself more—

Mr. Gaal: Oh, sure, and, of course, my wife has noticed the difference in me. She said to me last night (he grins sheepishly), "Whatever is happening to you, I like it." I guess the thing that really made it tough for me was that I never had a chance to tell that teacher how I felt about him. When I found out he was killed in Korea, well—ah—I hate to say it —but I was almost glad. Now, I know it isn't right to feel that way—oh, I was sorry about it—now, I think I am mostly sorry for him, but I've been all mixd up about it.

Pastor: You have been ashamed of hating him, but mostly frustrated that you haven't been able to let him know how you felt, and—

Mr. Gaal: Exactly. It's ridiculous that I have kept this thing buried for so long. It's sure helping to face up to it, which I have been avoiding all these years. I was too ashamed even to tell my wife about that thing. I thought, "Well, that's just kid stuff. I've outgrown that." I'll admit it has kind of flashed back a few times. I mean I remembered it, but I just sorta dismissed it from my mind. I guess I was more affected by those experiences than I thought.

Pastor: Apparently you are quite aware of how this pattern has been working in you.

Mr. Gaal: Yeah, I've been kicking him in the hind end all along. But I haven't been able to trust my feelings. You know, trying to be a nice guy—protecting that old salesman image! (He shoves his fist forward, cocks his head, winks his eye, and makes a popping sound with his mouth.) What a sham! What a damn sham! (He pauses.) You know, I feel better, I feel a *lot* better.

While I do not intend to give the impression of a "living happily ever after" ending to this story, the fact is that Mr. Gaal began to trust his feelings sufficiently to consent to becoming a father. About a year following the fore-going series of interviews, the pastor learned that Mr. Gaal and his wife had become parents of a son. This episode is recounted here because his acceptance of his son in truth symbolized his own self-acceptance.

In the portion of the interview given above, Mr. Gaal had begun to consolidate the data which were coming from his intensive inquiry into the "why's" of his be-havior.

He was integrating these data and realizing a strength-ened self-concept. This was not merely a matter of insight for him, but of *experiencing the reality of change while it was occurring.* He was consolidating his gains in self-understanding by becoming more discriminating about the judgments he was receiving from others and bringing such awareness in touch with his own feelings. Thus, he no longer assumed he would inevitably lose control of himself.

The conjunctive stage is also one in which the person becomes discerning about what he can learn from negative as well as positive experiences. Suffering, for example, can be a form of judgment. If it is sharply discerned, suffering can be seen in its creative as well as destructive dynamics. In this stage of the assimilative process, a person may be-come more discerning of the neurotic as distinguished from constructive ways of handling suffering. He now is begin-ning to comprehend to a significant degree the relation-ship of his suffering to the stubbornness of his evil will. This awakening tends to open the way to a transformation of his will, to a relaxation of his overwhelming demands from life, and to his acceptance of acceptance.

Mrs. Bimm, a housewife in her late thirties, was strug-gling through this stage during her third and fourth interviews. The following is a bit of the middle portion of the fourth interview:

Mrs. Bimm: I think probably that one of the deepest ties I have to my husband is that (she weeps) I've been more able with him—throughout all of these years, together—to be myself—ah—to say what I thought and even be unpleasant about it, if I felt like it. He has been very accepting. Despite all I've said in a derrogatory way about him, I must say in his favor, he's been very accepting. Only I think I fell into the trap when this sexual business arose—again seeing his problem and his need, you know—and falling into this family pattern of mine—of reaction, you know—and I shouldn't have. I know that now. (She weeps.)

Pastor: You are disappointed in yourself—that you don't act in your best knowledge—and you blame yourself for not being able to free yourself from this family attitude toward sex, and—

Mrs. Bimm: —accepting something that I shouldn't have accepted. But then I haven't been honest with him about this and I want to be. I want to straighten this out.

Pastor: All in all, you are saying, "Here is a relationship in which I am able, as nearly as I know, to be myself and really be spontaneous, even to the point of expressing negative feelings—and have them accepted." And although the sexual area is frustrating to you, you are finding that in many important ways he means more to you than you have realized.

Mrs. Bimm: Yeah. (She weeps.)

In this particular excerpt, Mrs. Bimm demonstrates how she was bringing together negative judgments about herself and positive judgments regarding her husband with her changing self-concept. Previously, she had expressed only anger and bitter feelings. Now she was dealing with the other side, not just in compensation, but in a genuine effort to be just and fair in her appraisal. Therefore, she was in the act of consolidating the gains she had made in understanding the situation, by pulling together the insights which had come to her in the preceding interviews.

Mrs. Bimm's suffering has been redemptive in that through it she has learned precisely how her husband feels. She resented him deeply for not confronting her when she was abusing him. "Why does he let me degrade him?" she cried. "I don't want to do that, but he infuriates me by just tolerating me," she had said at one point earlier in her counseling with the pastor. "Doesn't how I feel toward him make any difference?"

Although she is not yet able to regard his sexual approaches to her as anything other than hostile acts—"these attitudes have been so ingrained in me by my family"—she is discerning that his general acceptance of her is extremely important to her. Instead of condemning him in a wholesale fashion for his ineptitude in breaking down her defensiveness in sexual matters, she separates out her feelings and finds considerable warmth for him. Following the above interchange, she spoke hopefully of changes in her sexual attitudes, saying, "I think I have had difficulty accepting myself as a woman, but I have a feeling this is changing, too."

Basically Mrs. Bimm was struggling to discern how responsible to her husband she should really be in the face of what she felt was his indifference to her. How much could or should she give of herself, she had wondered. To what degree could or should she become involved in her husband's suffering? She recognized she depended almost entirely upon him for emotional support. Yet she was not meeting his needs and felt guilty about drawing upon him and giving little in return. She acknowledged her self-indulgent attitudes, she understood her husband's loneliness and consequent withdrawal from her, but she had not been able effectively to discipline herself to do anything about it.

Now she was beginning to interact with him instead of simply reacting to him. She found she could not demand love from him as a right, but must offer love as a gift. At every point where Mrs. Bimm contrasted herself with her husband she had felt thwarted, weak, unacceptable, dependent, and angry. In spite of the persistence of these feelings, which were heightened by her failures in the sexual relationship with her husband, she discovered that she was not weak, and that her husband was not the tower of strength she had supposed. Now she was getting a more realistic view of both herself and her husband as she began to bind together positive experiences with her feelings about herself.

A clue to the conjunctive or consolidating stage is seen in the person's resistance to bringing out new material in the counseling session. He seems to be saying, "Don't push me. I am content to remain here for a while to think about what is happening." This stage, thus, may be a temporary plateau in the whole process, but usually is not more than that, because the person has yet to put into action what he is learning from judgment. He will soon discover that integrating the data from judgment is not enough. He must test out and rework what he has learned until it becomes a veritable part of him. Otherwise, judgment has not performed its proper function. Nothing is drastically changed. He has not fully responded to this opportunity for growth.

The *conjunctive* stage is that in which the consolidation of gains in understanding begins to take place. This is the action of bringing experiences and feelings together, achieving a degree of congruence, and getting a different perspective on one's self and his situation. One becomes discriminating about what is negative as well as positive in the judgment he is experiencing and sees himself more realistically in relation to both.

7   Becoming a Self

Each step in the assimilation process serves to give sharper definition to the ego. The stage in which the person demonstrates he is coming to a conscious recognition of this fact is called *differentiation*. He is becoming discriminating of shades of differences between himself and others in regard to images, language, anxieties, etc., and is developing an understanding and appreciation of those differences. He is beginning to appreciate and to affirm his uniqueness. The more he distinguishes the "otherness" of the others, the more his own ego takes on character. The person is sharpening his awareness of the "thou" character of the other persons he encounters; consequently, he is enhancing the "I" character of his own selfhood. This differentiation process is similar to what Carl Gustav Jung has called "individuation." He defines the term as representing "the development of the psychological individual as a differentiated being from the general, collective psychology."[1] In another of his works he develops the concept further: "This natural process of individuation served me both as a model and guiding principle for my method of treatment. *The unconscious compensation of a neurotic conscious attitude contains all the elements that could effectively and*

[1] *Psychological Types* (New York: Pantheon Books, 1959), p. 561.

healthily correct the one-sidedness of the conscious mind, if these elements were made conscious, i.e., understood and integrated into it as realities" [2] (italics mine). This is precisely what I see as the function of judgment. To translate: Judgment from the self, others, and God "contains all the elements that could effectively and healthily correct the one-sidedness" of the self, if these elements were "understood and integrated" (or assimilated) into the total self.

The critical difference between our points of view, as I see it, is: Jung was speaking psychologically of the assimilation of data from the collective unconscious, while I am speaking, theologically, of the assimilation of the data of judgment from the various sources—the ethically and morally judging self, the judging community, and the judging God, under whom all are judged. I contend that I am regarding social interaction as of greater consequence to the developing ego than Jung explicitly recognizes. Furthermore, I maintain that the theological context of judgment is always implicitly present and should be discerned explicitly. The latter requires continuous dialogue in which ultimate concerns are the specific subject matter.

Having earlier acknowledged his indebtedness to Martin Buber, who set forth the dialogical theme of interpersonal encounter in his classic work *I and Thou*. Reinhold Niebuhr puts the basic dynamism of the stage of differentiation, as I am interpreting it, into theological language as follows:

Our approach to other human personalities offers an illuminating analogy of the necessity and character of "revelation" in our relation to God. We have various evidence that, when

[2] *Two Essays in Analytical Psychology* (New York: Pantheon Books, 1959), pp. 108-9.

89

dealing with persons, we are confronting a reality of greater depth than the mere organism of animal life. We have evidence that we are dealing with a "Thou" of such freedom and uniqueness that a mere external observation of its behavior will not only leave the final essence of that person obscure but will actually falsify it, since such observation would debase what is really free subject into a mere object. This person, this other "Thou" cannot be understood until he speaks to us; until his behavior is clarified by the "word" which comes out of the ultimate and transcendent unity of his spirit. Only such a word can give us the key by which we understand the complexities of his behavior. This word spoken from beyond us and to us is both a verification of our belief that we are dealing with a different dimension than animal existence; and also a revelation of the actual and precise character of the person with whom we are dealing.[3]

The latter phrases really describe what is meant by the stage of differentiation. The person sees the freedom and uniqueness of the person to whom he is relating and begins really "to understand the complexities of his behavior" and, at the same time, to become more discerning of the complexities of his own. But this must be regarded as an awakening, not a full-blown response, to the "thou" of the other, which continues to remain, at least in part, a mystery.

Equally true is his awareness of the "I" of himself, which is given content, meaning, and distinctiveness by the very encounter with the "thou" of the other. Even this is insufficient, however, to get a perspective upon the real strengths and weaknesses of the "I." Until one confronts the "thou" in the universe, the revealed yet hidden mystery of being itself, one has yet to bring the "I" into sharper focus.

[3] *The Nature and Destiny of Man* (New York: Charles Scribner's Sons, 1946), I, 130.

The "I," thus, also becomes revealed yet remains, in part, a mystery in the very act of confronting judgment from the various sources. As the person becomes more differentiated, his capacity for assimilating judgment is increased. Paradoxically, while the person is gaining in his appreciation of the "thou" character of other persons, he is greatly enchancing the "I" character of himself. The dynamic and even the order of the process is summed up in what has been called the Great Commandment: "You shall love the Lord your God with all your heart, and with all your soul, and with all your mind. This is the great and first Commandment. And a second is like it, you shall love your neighbor as yourself" (Matt. 22:36-39). Stated here is the action required to develop acuity of judgment, by which distorted images and perceptions are cleared up and one knows "even as he is known." As the apostle Paul articulates his conviction regarding the ultimate goal, "Now I know in part; then I shall understand fully, even as I have been fully understood" (I Cor. 13:12b). The meaning here is not merely revelation at the end of history, but also realization within time of the quality of relationships in which love operates.

Differences between persons and groups provide variety and interest to life, on the one hand, and intensify encounters between them, on the other. Out of such encounters is born the uniqueness and remarkable contrasts which give character to existence. Otherwise, existence would meld into a colorless blob. As one provokes support, moves with, and moves against the other, he evokes that person into being. In turn, he is called into a uniqueness which is power and creativity. As the person cherishes the distinctness of the other, he adds immeasurably to his own distinction. By the same token, if he truly can succeed in destroying the distinctiveness of the other, he has, by the same act, destroyed his own.

Differentiation is the act, therefore, of becoming "as a part," by affirming the distinctiveness of the other, thus affirming the distinctiveness of oneself. Paul Tillich has argued for the fundamental unity of this process:

> The courage to be as a part is an integral element of the courage to be as oneself, and the courage to be as oneself is an integral element of the courage to be as a part. But under the conditions of human finitude and estrangement that which is essentially united becomes existentially split. The courage to be as a part separates itself from unity with the courage to be as oneself, and conversely; and both disintegrate in their isolation.[4]

I am talking about the uniting direction of this process which Tillich discusses later in *The Courage to Be,* under the section of which the theme is: the courage to accept acceptance. I intend later, also, to show that true differentiation requires the dialectical phase of the total process, in which ultimate dimensions of differentiation are recognized.

To show how one person experienced the stage of differentiation, I cite the following excerpt from a group session.

The group consisted of eight men, all of whom were ministers. They were largely middle-aged and had been graduated from seminaries a number of years previously. All were serving local parishes. The leader of the group was a man who was serving a church in a specialized counseling ministry. He had been trained in centers for clinical pastoral education and in other specialized training centers.

[4] *The Courage to Be,* p. 90.

This information is important to this case study because knowledge of the leader's training served as a barrier to the key person's participation.

After four days of what was to be a two-week period of intensive study and encounter, Mr. Radd drew the group leader aside and asked for an individual session. The leader met Mr. Radd the following day. Mr. Radd was an average-sized, serious-looking man who rarely smiled either in the group sessions or outside them. He simply said to the group leader, "I am hurting, and I want to do something about it." He went on to say that he had almost canceled out after the first few days. He had felt the antithetical character of judgment and was not sure he could withstand it. "I don't mean to imply the fellows have been hard on me. They actually haven't. In fact, that's part of the problem. I am being ignored. That's harder to take. Whenever I say anything, the other members look at me for a moment, then proceed to something else. What's the matter with me that I can't express myself so they'll take notice of it? What do these guys see in me that they don't like—if that's it?" He was at the interrogatory stage.

"Apparently you would really like members of the group to tell you how they see you, is that it?"

"Yes, I guess I would."

"Why not bring your feelings out in the group session?"

"I don't know whether I can or not."

"Whether you are ready to trust the members of the group enough yet to do so?"

"Maybe that's it, I don't know."

The following day (Friday) several members of the group began to evaluate the week's experience. Jack, the most articulate member, was saying he was "more threatened, consequently more conscious of Ted and Bill than of

93

any others," because he felt they were perhaps better informed about many of the subjects under discussion. Ted stated he had immediately felt angry with Jack because he sensed Jack had set out to snatch the leader's role and he was disappointed with George (Mr. Radd), who he felt was tacitly consenting to Jack's planned coup. "Furthermore, George," he said directly to Mr. Radd, "you never seem to be listening when someone other than Jack speaks. And when anyone speaks to you, you interrupt before he can say what he had to say."

"Why do you find it so important to take over this group?" Ted questioned Jack point-blank.

"So you won't," Jack laughingly fired back without hesitation. All other members of the group laughed except Mr. Radd, whose expression at that point was quizzical. He had not heard anything beyond Ted's statement identifying him with Jack.

Again he talked with the leader. The judgment of which he had become aware was: he denied his own strength. He identified with the strongest person in the group to bolster his own ego. He did not trust the leader, because he had a habit of not trusting persons in positions of authority. He was always defending what he believed because "I guess I am not sure I really believe it. I am not coming out with my feelings in this group. I never do. I find you just don't dare let the people in these church groups know how you really feel. They can't stand for you to be human." He went away from his conversation with the group leader "shaken but somewhat relieved."

When the group met the following week, Mr. Radd began to participate. About halfway through the session Bill observed: "George, you seem to be more relaxed today."

"Well, I am. I've done a lot of thinking this weekend. Ted is right. I haven't really been listening to you. I have been so busy over here defending my theology and being preoccupied with my own thoughts, I haven't been hearing you. I feel a lot better today."

"You come through better," Ted quickly responded.

Three days later Mr. Radd came to the group leader smiling broadly: "The tension seems to be all gone," he said. "I started this group like I do most groups—all tense and braced up—like I was ready to fight the world. Now, I don't need to. (He gestured by opening his arms wide.) I'm getting a new look at myself. I hope I can hold this feeling! It's a good feeling! I don't have to worry about whether or not what I say to these guys is right. I find they're not concerned about that either."

Mr. Radd is now manifesting what may be regarded as a beginning consciousness of the stage of differentiation. He can dare to be himself, and he can dare to be a part of the group. Previously, he was hamstrung by his fears and could be neither. The acceptance is not purely from the group, as we will note later, but is beyond the group and enables members of the group to share it.

Mr. Radd will undoubtedly find he can now proceed to the stage of differentiation more rapidly in any group in which he participates. He has had an experience which has added great strength to his capacity for differentiation. Although he probably will not be entirely free from anxiety in each new group situation—nor should he be, for anxiety, indeed, keeps him honest in such situations—such anxiety as will arise probably will not deter him from repeated efforts at participation.

At the end of the period of meeting together, the group evaluated the whole experience. Mr. Radd confessed he had been extremely apprehensive during the early sessions. He said he was defensive about his theology because some members of the group had immediately offended him. He was happy to realize his opinion of them had become favorable—that he could accept their differences from him. He found he could risk his theological position. In fact, he discovered it really supported him in many helpful ways.

"You don't realize how much these few days have meant to me," he said to the leader after the final group session. "My views have been strengthened, because I have found out in this group what my theology really means to me. Before, when I found myself outside of my own denominational group and saw that great theological differences existed, I wouldn't even express myself. I just avoided discussing issues with other people. Here in this group I have felt free to say a lot of things I would never have dreamed I could. I have learned a lot. I just hope I can keep on."

Differentiation for Mr. Radd was precisely the act of appreciating the differences of the other men in the group —consequently getting a greater appreciation of his own theological orientation. He was "loosening up," as he put it, but he saw this development in himself realistically, not as compromising his beliefs, but as giving them sharpness and clarity.

Mr. Radd was beginning to stand out in the group—to take on character. He was awakening to the realization that his background served him as a resource rather than a fortress. He was becoming more discriminating as to particular ways his theological position was vulnerable, but this did not threaten him, because he was also learning its strengths, thus he could gain as well as give ground, hence did not have to be primarily on the defensive.

On the whole, Mr. Radd was greatly encouraged to discover his personal strength in the group. Whereas he had been one of the "faceless ones" at the time of the group's first efforts at evaluation, at the final evaluation he was pleased to learn he was being recognized by members of the group.

Differentiation thus is the act of discovering oneself through becoming discerningly conscious of the phenomenology of others and consequently more accurately in touch with one's own phenomenology. The "individuation" here is in the act of daring to stand out, or as we have observed in Tillich's words, "the courage to be as oneself" uniting with "the courage to be as a part." A person thus becomes enabled to become more discerning as to his particular strengths and weaknesses and to risk both in encounter with others.

Becoming a self requires the process of *differentiation*. Differentiation is the act of affirming one's own and others' differences. The courage to be as oneself and the courage to be as a part are united in this stage. A person stands out in the group. He is becoming discriminating of who he is and whence he came. He is able to appropriate aspects of his own background discerningly, and is, to a degree at least, conscious of the nature of his conflict with it. His assimilation of judgment at this point helps him to distinguish his identity.

8   Testing Out

The stage of *experimentation* is reached when the person attempts to verify his personal gains by testing them in concrete situations. He is actually assessing the reliability of his developing discernment by validating his judgments in interpersonal and group situations. He becomes his own "participant observer." He is perhaps as painfully conscious of his performance as any learner attempting to apply what he knows about a skill. This is the process of translating what already has been assimilated from judgment into revised action. This stage, therefore, represents a further consolidation of gains in self-judgment through trial and error participation in intensive interpersonal interactions.

This testing stage is essential to the assimilation process because it represents the implementation of revised views derived from the encounter with judgment. It is a necessary step in learning from any experience. Experimentation with one's changing concepts takes more time—possibly more than any other stage—because the person must have opportunity to validate what he is learning in different situations. As he becomes convinced of his effectiveness in each situation, he operates less self-consciously and with confidence in his capacity to achieve his goals.

The chief mode of operating within this stage is to test

or try out one's revised or refined judgments in situations where he once responded in an inadequate, inappropriate, or inefficient manner. In the counseling relationships, when a person changes his judgments or perceptions of judgments in another, he returns to relate to that other person, testing out his revised notions.

We may illustrate this phase of the assimilation process by citing the following interchange between the pastor and Miss Linn, a twenty-three-year-old college student and part-time employee in the business office of a nearby hospital. Her older sister worked in another department of the same hospital. The two young women lived together in an apartment just off the campus, an arrangement which they had maintained since the beginning of Miss Linn's college career. Now in her senior year, Miss Linn was planning to marry her fiancé upon graduation, but she was so apprehensive about her forthcoming marriage that she initiated the counseling relationship with the pastor.

She immediately brought out her concern about the psychological health of her relationship with her fiancé. She was aware that she tended to "lean on him too much"— that she was attracted to him in the first place because of his poise in social situations, a strength which she felt she lacked. She had become quite anxious about entering into the marriage, realizing she was perpetuating a pattern of "unwholesomeness" about which she was becoming increasingly concerned, namely, an extreme submissiveness and indecisiveness in all her relationships. She was alarmed about her dependency needs which, she said, she felt helpless to change. "I am caught in a vicious cycle," she acknowledged.

In the interrogatory stage Miss Linn came to the conclusion she could begin to do something in relation to her sister. "Here is one relationship which I can start on," she said. She eventually saw how she was permitting her sister to dominate her and make decisions for her. "I consult her on everything," she said, "from clothing to boy friends." She felt so obligated to her sister, she added, that she did not dare say anything contrary to her sister's views or stand up to her in any way. The net result, she observed, was that she was existing in an intolerably overcontrolled situation, which she feared might break open at any time.

Once she had reflected upon the pattern of her relationship with her sister, and had seen how typical it was of her more intimate relationships with people, Miss Linn concluded that she must take the risk of really confronting her sister. The result gave her a mild shock. The following excerpt is from the interview which followed, about a week later.

Miss Linn: You remember I told you I had made up my mind to speak up to my sister and let her know how I feel about things, well, I did that one night last week (exultantly), and you should have seen her face. Was she surprised! You could have knocked her over with a feather. But, you know, that was one of the most rewarding evenings I ever had. I discovered how human my sister really is. She was warm and tender—ah—sympathetic. For the first time, I was able to talk with her about my doubts regarding Larry. Then, to top it off, she confided in me about the man she had been dating. I didn't even know he was a married man! She had been hiding her feelings from me, and I didn't realize how torn up she's really been. She seemed to appreciate talking with me and—well—it seems like everything's changed between us—and we've really been getting acquainted this past week. It's—oh—it's real good. (She ges-

tures with her hands as if to imply, "What more can I say?")
Pastor: It's wonderful to discover your sister this way—to find she's a human being, too. You are experiencing a kind of a victory, too—being able to act on the resolution that you made last week.
Miss Linn: Yes, but I haven't told you the most encouraging part yet. I found myself taking part in the discussion in the meeting of our group last week. The other members of the group responded to what I said in a way I don't remember ever experiencing. What thrilled me most, though, was afterwards when Larry told me how proud he was of me.

The nature of the experimentation here is self-evident. Miss Linn had tested her insights into her own strengths and weakness in her relationship with her sister and discovered that she was functioning more effectively than she had even believed she could. Her success carried over into a social situation, where she surprised herself and those who had known her by speaking out quite informedly on the subject under discussion. Her growing awareness that she had for some time been living symbiotically through her sister and others was the beginning of differentiation which she was now trying out in several concrete situations.

A goal of the person in the stage of experimentation is that of testing out his power and effectiveness in relation to persons and groups. He may be as fearful of his newfound power as he was previously of his impotency. Thus, he must live with the experiencing of power for a time to get a perspective upon it.

Mr. Watt, for example, had come to what he described as a "dead spot" in his career. He talked with his pastor about feeling "left behind in the rush of rapid changes in our industry." Although he had been educated as an engineer, he was not actually working at an engineering job. For that reason, he said, he was unhappy with his present position and was not keeping up with his field. His presented problem was his relationship with his supervisor, who continually "bugged him" about each little job he did.

Briefly, as he made progress in his counseling, his evaluation of himself changed markedly. The remarkable side effect was a complete reversal of roles between the supervisor and himself. Mr. Watt was now having difficulty adapting himself to the consultant image into which the supervisor had placed him. "It just began to happen that way," Mr. Watt exclaimed with a shrug. "I have to test this out all the time, because I am never sure when he may put me in my place. I am not quarreling with the whole business right now, though," he grinned. "I am content to take it as it comes, which is a new way of operating for me."

Mr. Watt's experiencing of his own power was at once awkward and fulfilling to him. As he tested it out in the particular situation with his supervisors, he discovered he was carrying his effectiveness over into other relationships —with his wife, children, friends in the church, and so on. With considerable perception into his own dynamic processes, he recognized what was happening and specifically commented: "I am encouraged that I am moving off dead center. I was beginning to lose confidence in my ability. There was no need for that, but I really could not convince myself of it. A few successes in my relations with my associates the past few months have helped a great deal. I am a little awed at times, right now, with what I can do. I don't have to be ashamed of being proud of that anymore. Of course, I don't think there is much danger of getting too conceited. (He laughed.) I don't know! All I know is, I've never had that kind of problem, and I don't think I am going to now."

Erik Erikson sees the fundamental task of this stage as typical of an early developmental period in the life of the children; namely, *"mastery of the conflicts* which were projected on them and—the *prestige* gained through such mastery." [1] "This new mastery is not restricted to the technical mastery of toys and things," Erikson continues. "It also includes an infantile way of mastering *experience* by meditating, experimenting, planning, and sharing." This process is repeated in any new learning situation throughout childhood and into adult life. The conviction the child has at this stage in his development is, according to Erikson, "I am what I learn."

The person's "experimenting, planning, and sharing" actually characterizes the dynamic of the final three stages in the assimilation process. One tests out what he has learned, incorporates this into his planning, and as he experiences benefits, is eager to share the contributing experiences with others. We will say more about the latter in connection with the final stage, in which sharing plays an important role.

A decisive element in the completion of this stage is that of the teaching which follows the learning through experimentation. Nothing quite so firmly fixes the reality of what one has learned as the demand to teach it to another. When a person is forced to communicate his understanding of what he has come to know, he is provoked to present that knowledge so that it may mean as much to the learner as it has to him. Erikson again makes a helpful

[1] "Growth and Crises of the 'Healthy Personality,'" in Clyde Kluckhohn and Henry A. Murray, eds., *Personality in Nature, Society, and Culture* (New York: Alfred A. Knopf, 1954), p. 213.

observation: "And man *needs* to teach, not only for the sake of those who need to be taught, and not only for the fulfillment of his identity, but because facts are kept alive by being told, logic by being demonstrated, truth by being professed." [2] Testing out one's appropriation of judgment is heightened considerably by the assumption of teaching and leadership roles wherein the person confirms his capacity to take in judgment as well as to face new judgments.

In my previous discussion of the experience of George Radd in the group of his colleagues, I referred to his dynamics in the stage of differentiation. I now quote from the material which may be regarded as exemplifying the stage of experimentation. The following is a brief excerpt from the exchanges among the various members during one of the later sessions of the group.

George Radd: (He responds to a statement by Ted.) I'd like to hear from Ralph and Mark. They have obviously been reacting to what you say, Ted, but they haven't been saying anything.

Jack: Oh, so you want to take over the leadership of the group, do you, George?

George: Might as well. (He laughs.) Looks like everyone else is trying it. Why not take my turn? (They all laugh.)

Ted: Is that the way you see it, George, that we are all competing with each other to be the leader of the group?

George: Well, Ted, you'll have to admit you have been working pretty hard at it. (They glare at each other for a moment.)

Bob: I am beginning to get a different view of George. At first I didn't believe he had a thought of his own. Now I am beginning to get a lot of respect for him.

[2] *Insight and Responsibility* (New York: W. W. Norton & Co., 1964), p. 131.

George: (He has not taken his eyes off Jack.) Jack, I have had a feeling right along that you have been laughing at me.

Jack: Maybe I did, at first. In fact, my first impression of all you guys was that you were all gutless preachers who just were generally apologetic for who you were. I have found out you are all stronger than I gave you credit for.

George: Magnanimous of you, old chap! I think I speak for several of the guys when I say we were having a devil of a time accepting you, too, but you finally gave up your "God" role, and we decided we could live with you. (They all laugh.)

Mr. Radd had indeed temporarily assumed a leadership role. Yet he had not felt guilty about doing so. He did not look continually at the leader for approval of his presumptive act. Furthermore, he did not feel that he was showing disrespect for the leader. In fact, he confessed to the leader at the conclusion of the sessions that he would have had neither "the courage, the strength, nor the audacity" to have stepped into "even a brief moment of leadership" had he not developed tremendous respect for the leader of the group. It was this very developing respect, he declared, which had given him the support he needed to try out the leader role. "I have never done this in a group," he said. "It is a new and exciting experience for me. The guys attacked me pretty hard. If anyone had told me how it would be, I wouldn't have come! I didn't feel annihilated, though—and that's the difference." Mr. Radd's experimentation had taught him he could risk himself and survive!

Perhaps the most difficult discipline in the whole of the assimilation process is required in the stage of experimentation. Decisiveness, patience, and persistence, all of which have presumably been strengthened in experiences within the earlier stages of the assimilation process, go into completing this stage. As I have implied, the importance of reinforcement from an ally or allies is clearly indicated. We will talk later about how the supportive community is of critical significance to this stage. The church, for example, ideally engenders faith through faith which is visible, concrete, and specifically relevant to particular needs.

Testing out is an action phase of the assimilation process. Through *experimentation* one implements the judgment he is taking in and incorporating. The person's power and effectiveness in relationships are tested. Support and reinforcement from other persons and from groups are essential to this stage, because acceptance of both successes and failures is essential. Teaching as well as learning intensifies the assimilation process, because teaching can supply specific motivation to master the experience and to develop the imaginative processes required to communicate what one has learned.

9 Achieving a New Perspective

Having tested in concrete relationships what he is assimilating of judgment from various sources, the person is ready to turn his attention to the larger context of meaning of which he is relatively aware. He is at the point of conceptualizing—interpreting what he is experiencing. The dynamic of this stage may be described as *dialectical*. The dialogue is with God. Specifically, I am referring to the person's acknowledgment of what he is experiencing as the confrontation of God's judgment. The term "dialectic" best conveys the nature of the engagement. The person is now becoming consciously involved in an encounter with God. He sees himself judged in ultimate terms. He may not use "God-talk" to symbolize this experiencing of ultimate judgment, but he will use language which expresses his own awareness of the ultimate dimensions of his concern.

However he interprets and symbolizes the inherent push within him to gain ultimate understanding and perspective on his existence, it is a life and death matter to him. Through both his successes and failures in his assimilation of judgment he confronts God. Such encounter is necessary to the development of his true powers of discrimination. He is at once humbled and exalted in the confrontation. He is humbled in that his best judgments are judged

("I will destroy the wisdom of the wise"—I Cor. 1:19); he is exalted in the sense of being led through his judgments to a fulfillment which transcends them.

Through his dialogue with God, a person's capacity for perceiving truth and error is sharpened. He faces up to having his proximate judgments judged, but in this receives a judgment which saves him. This truth is at the heart of spiritual discipline, and is what truly gives man spirit. He is chastened, but it is in the spirit of love, not rejection. His perspective is enlarged, and through the purging power of God's judgment he is opened to an awareness and acceptance of the grace and mercy of God.

The person is now realizing that, although at times God stands sharply against him, God is neither alien nor lacking in compassion. On the contrary, as Daniel Day Williams asserts,

When we recognize the self-giving love of Christ we accept his judgment against our lovelessness. . . . The New Testament meets the problem of our guilt at a point which [theories of atonement] all tend to miss, *the personal experience of forgiveness.* . . . The person who cannot solve his own problems discovers one who will stand by him in spite of his burden of guilt or fear, whatever it may be. The person who is accepted does not earn this. He has no claim upon it. It is offered. It is grace." [1]

In this discussion of the assimilation of judgment we have come full circle, or to use a better metaphor, we have finally turned over the coin to see what is on the other side. We acknowledge the other side as grace. The real dynamic of the dialectical stage, therefore, is the dialectic

[1] *The Minister and the Care of Souls.* (New York: Harper Brothers, 1961), p. 88. Italics mine.

between judgment and grace. The person is aware that he has received an unmerited gift in the "judgment against his lovelessness." He is conscious of acceptance which he has not earned.

"When we speak of Christ's suffering as a disclosure of the spirit of God," Williams says at another point, "we go beyond what any human experience can prove, but we find analogies in experience which become luminous in the life of faith. We see why the New Testament asserts that we cannot know the love of God except as it is first given to us in our brokenness." [2] I quote this because I regard it as an excellent word with which to introduce the following illustration of the reality to which Williams points.

The pastor had been seeing Mr. Bronn in counseling sessions over a period of several months. Mr. Bronn was a college educated, skilled laborer, about forty-two years of age. He was married and the father of two young children. His wife was employed in the office of a company near their home. She was highly efficient in the office, but, by admission of both of them, "a very poor housekeeper." Also, they both claimed they were sexually incompatible, and each felt the other was largely at fault. He was suspicious of any interest she manifested toward the men in her office.

In the early interviews Mr. Bronn displayed considerable anxiety. One could detect even obvious physiological signs, such as prominent red blotches on his neck which were even more pronounced against his blanched face. At each session he made a ritual of turning his chair away from that of the counselor and placing it so he faced the window. Thus he took a position slightly askance from the counselor, with whom he talked by turning his head toward

[2] *Ibid.*, p. 91.

the pastor just enough to be heard. His mood, during the early sessions, was primarily depressed. He kept his head lowered and spoke quietly, almost apologetically. He gave the general impression of sadness and defeat. He rarely smiled, but his affective responses were varied.

He struggled through the earlier stages of the assimilation process, acknowledging he had learned much about himself—his defenses, etc. Throughout the early sessions he confessed a period of unfaithfulness to his wife, discussed embarrassing vocational failures, and bemoaned his inability to be effective generally in interpersonal relationships. One of his previous counselors (there were several), he said, told him he was trying to prove to himself he was a man. He admitted the observation was probably correct but said now that he knew that, what was he to do about it?

After a number of sessions in which he seemed to wish to explore every twist and turn of his own complicated behavior patterns, he came to see the pastor saying, "I almost canceled out today, but decided I'd better come on in." At about the midpoint of that interview, Mr. Bronn suddenly, but quietly, stood up as if to leave. The pastor, assuming that he was indeed preparing to leave, also rose from his chair. Instead of leaving, however, Mr. Bronn picked up his chair, deliberately turned it toward the pastor's chair, emphatically placed it in a position directly facing the pastor, and sat down again. Seeing immediately what Mr. Bronn was doing, the pastor sat down in his own chair. Mr. Bronn looked into the face of the counselor, drew a deep breath, and began to speak.

Mr. Bronn: It's strange, but I feel forgiven! (He pauses as the counselor nods his head. He is obviously relaxed. The physi-

110

ological manifestations have disappeared entirely. His face appears a bit flushed.) Obviously, I haven't done anything to you to need forgiving for, so you aren't the one who has done the forgiving—oh, hell, maybe you have, too, I don't know. I don't know how to explain it! I've never been able to get off my own back, so I know it isn't me. (He points vigorously at his chest and speaks emphatically.) *I just feel forgiven!*

Pastor: Suddenly you feel that you are accepted—

Mr. Bronn: I don't know what you mean by that, but I do know I feel forgiven, and I just now said, "Boy, this is silly. Me here sitting, looking out the window. I can face that guy. He's my friend. He's not going to tell me to go to hell." But it's not you, like I said. Why should I be afraid to face you? I haven't done anything to you that I know of. Oh, I guess I have been scared you were going to condemn me for what I've been doing. I'll tell you right now, though, I've been harder on myself than you've been on me. Maybe that's it! You've helped me to see that God don't hold it against me. I've been finding out I'm not satisfied to excuse what I can get by with. There's something else. I thought I was free from all this "God-stuff." I'm not so sure—ah—I don't know what to think about it. Maybe I was so brainwashed with religious gobbledegook when I was a child, I just can't get away from it. I don't think that's it, though. I'm finding out I can't have life just the way *I* want it. Every time I try, I seem to run into myself. Or, I've thought it's me I was running into—maybe it's God. What a horrible thought!

Pastor: A horrible thought? (He was undoubtedly shocked by the phrase.)

Mr. Bronn: Yes—I mean, to realize that I was just kidding myself in thinking I was emancipated from my narrow religious background.

Pastor: You are saying you fear perhaps you are caught in

your former religious patterns of thinking and putting that kind of twist on what you are facing now?

Mr. Bronn: Yeah, maybe, but I don't think so. It isn't the same. I just see it differently, that's all. Maybe I just can't escape God, or something like it, I don't know. But the point is, I no longer feel I have to. I don't want to run anymore. I want to square off. I am not afraid of it, now. (He had demonstrated what he was communicating here by his act of deliberately moving his chair into a vis-à-vis position before the pastor.)

Pastor: You have the courage now to face me—for that matter, the courage to face anyone, even God, if that's what it means.

Mr. Bronn: That's right. But it isn't that I think I'm so great. I'm not kidding myself, or you either. I've just been doing a hell of a lot better lately, and I can lift my head up for a change. I don't know why you've stuck with me, sometimes, but you have, and that means a lot. I can't put my finger on what's happened, but that doesn't bother me too much. I am not so all-fired down on myself like I was—that's hell! I have had enough of that. I think I'm beginning to understand more about a lot of things, and—I'm not so worried about what I don't know.

Mr. Bronn was articulating what he was experiencing as forgiveness. Had anyone at any point in the counseling relationship told him this is what he should expect, he undoubtedly would have been unable either to understand or accept it. He was involved in his own dialectical encounter and enjoying the excitement of it. Although he was not using the words, he was understanding the relationship between judgment and grace. He actually perceived that relationship in his own experience.

In the dialectical stage, the person embodies the tension which is represented externally as the continuing dialogue between psychology and theology. Have I been implying throughout this discussion that all experiences must ultimately be interpreted in terms of theological categories? Not at all. However, I am saying theological implications are there and, for judgment to do its work, must eventually be considered. Yet love and *kairos* ("love at the right time") are integral to the dialectical encounter.

Daniel Day Williams raises the question: "Indeed do we not need to explain the fact that many sick persons will be positively harmed if they are confronted with the sheer declaration of God's judgment and his forgiveness?" [3] We have seen such recognition come only after a relatively long process of the assimilation of judgment. The person sees and knows because he is able to discern analogously what is meant by drawing upon his immediate experience.

Williams continues, "The religious discussion of guilt may prevent a person from taking a first step toward dealing with his personal guilt feelings. His repressed guilt may be too shattering to be borne *without a long preparation in the accepting situation*." [4]

Williams says that these may sound like convincing arguments for keeping theological and medical and psychological problems of persons quite apart. On the contrary, he affirms the involvement of each with the other, stating that a dialectical relationship is needed. For example, he maintains, "The mystery of atonement can be approached with new understanding if theology and psychology will look together at the same reality, however difficult it may be to do so." [5]

Putting Williams' statement a bit differently to connote

[3] *Ibid.*, p. 79.
[4] *Ibid.*
[5] *Ibid.*, p. 80.

what is precisely meant in this stage: The person has come to the place in his assimilation of judgment where he must look at the same reality of his experiencing from both a psychological and a theological perspective, however difficult it may be to maintain that dialectical encounter within himself and in relation to others.

The *dialectical* stage marks the achievement of a new perspective upon one's self and one's experiencing. Herein the chief mode of operation is to engage in a dialogue in which ultimate dimensions of judgment are acknowledged and considered. Although the person may not use "religious" language to carry on the dialogue, he is aware of ultimate implications of the judgment he is assimilating. For example, he begins to comprehend the grace in forgiveness. Each confrontation in which he experiences judgment affords the person the opportunity to add content to the dialogue and to test out the reality of that content in his relationships. The person must embody the dialectic which keeps him open to new occasions for judgment.

10　Toward Transformation

The final stage in the process of the assimilation of judgment is called *metamorphic,* because it signifies a transformation of the self. The data being assimilated are becoming a part of one. His actions flow from his revised being and are consistent with it. The person is obviously changing. He is aware of the change and so are others who observe him. A true metamorphosis has occurred. He is a "new creation." The old, in some sense, has passed away. (I qualify the statement to avoid suggesting there is no continuity between what he was and what he now is.) He acts in terms of the new creation he is becoming.

The word "transformation" seems particularly appropriate to this stage because it accurately symbolizes what is occurring. The apostle Paul actually used the term to speak of the discipline essential to the Christian life: "Do not be conformed to this world but be transformed (*metamorphousthe*) by the renewal of your mind (*nous*), that you may prove what is the will of God, what is good and acceptable and perfect" (Rom. 12:2).

Transformation, as we have sought to show, is indeed effected by the renewal of the mind, especially when this means a revised understanding through the confrontation of judgment. In its particular application to the assimilation process, *transformation occurs through the re-*

115

newal of the mind as the self risks itself in encounter and incorporates the judgment which it experiences in that encounter.

This is clearly within the intent of the total context of the foregoing passage from the twelfth chapter of Romans: "For by grace given to me I bid every one among you not to think of himself more highly than he ought to think, but to think with *sober judgment,* each according to the measure of faith which God has assigned him" (Rom. 12:3, italics mine). To the degree one can, in his maturity of faith, be discriminating in his judgments, he should evaluate himself appropriately. To be continually self-effacing is one form of pride, while being arrogant and haughty is another. Being always on the defensive is to close one's self off so that disclosure of the revealed yet hidden meanings cannot occur.

In this metamorphic stage, the person acts in concert with his growing appreciation of the ultimate dimensions of judgment and grace. He is translating these understandings into decisive actions. He finds he does so spontaneously and is usually surprised at his increased ability to do so. He is neither as impressed with his newfound power nor as frightened of it as he thought he would be, when he previously anticipated the possibility.

The stage of metamorphosis, or transformation, is shown in the following interview. The interview represents a beginning phase of the stage for Mrs. Wenn. She later became quite active in mental health programs of the county in which she lived, and eventually became an employed professional worker in the county association for mental health. At the time of the interview she was in her middle forties, the mother of two adolescent boys, and the wife of a teacher in the public schools. She was completing a Master of Arts degree in one of the local universities. Prior to this interview she had been in counseling with the pastor for more than a year.

Mrs. Wenn: Did I tell you that I have enrolled in the Wednesday evening Bible class over at the church?

Pastor: No, I don't recall your telling me that.

Mrs. Wenn: Well, last time I realized I am really so far behind and know so little (she laughs)—maybe that's why I think so deep, because now I am beginning to know where I am— I mean where I'm not! Oh, I think you know what I mean, but I'm not saying it (she laughs)—I am thrilled with what's opening up to me. Oh, I'm still not satisfied with the way things are, but I am not worrying so much—I'm beginning to understand more. It doesn't bother me that I still have problems. So-o (she draws the word out) I think it's going to be very interesting, and beneficial—ah—just to familiarize myself with the Bible, to study it again in a new light.

Pastor: You are thrilled by your new insight into the Bible and by what it is opening up to you in your—

Mrs. Wenn: Yes, I recognize that not long ago as I read the Bible, most of it didn't carry too much meaning for me at all, but now this feeling is being eradicated. Now in this class, we are supposed to go only until 9:15, but last time we didn't break up until 9:40 (she laughs), so you can see people are really enjoying it. I like to be in a group where everyone is interested. We were talking about the "new birth." I was particularly involved because that's what's happening to me. Oh—I certainly am a changed person. I don't know if it's as obvious to you as it is to me—but—

Pastor: Yes, I've been aware—

Mrs. Wenn: I certainly feel it. Ah—I suppose one of the things I've been wanting to say this afternoon is—ah—how grateful I am to you for what you have done for me.

Pastor: Thank you. It's been quite gratifying to see you making progress.

Mrs. Wenn: I know, but sometimes it hasn't been easy. And I know that this has bothered me for so long. Take going to church, for example. I would get up in the morning and get ready for church—and it was very much like when I first started coming to see you. As I got dressed I began to shake a little, pretty soon I began to shake a lot, and then I'd just let go. By the time I get here I'm a nervous wreck. But I make myself go. It's the same feeling going to church. Now, the last few Sundays I have experienced a peacefulness in the worship service, just like the comfortable feeling I have here. I enjoy the whole atmosphere, the music, the singing, the whole service. Like last Sunday, I found that I was listening —which is something I haven't been able to do—to what was going on. The sermon was real good and took me right out of myself.

Pastor: You are fascinated by your whole new discovery of what is going on outside of yourself.

Mrs. Wenn: You see, I have concentrated for so long in thinking about myself and my own problems—that it is almost like discovering a new world, and I am enjoying it.

Pastor: Like geting new life?

Mrs. Wenn: Oh, very much! Now even some of my fears have evaporated. I never could figure out why I was so afraid of death, for instance. I couldn't talk about it or face it in any way. I have even tried to pinpoint something in my childhood that made me this way, but I couldn't find any specific incident.

Pastor: You are deeply concerned about your fear of death?

Mrs. Wenn: Not any more. I mean, really as far as I am concerned, I am not afraid to die. I don't want to, of course, primarily because I have so much I want to do; but, I mean I can share my feelings openly with other people. Just this week I ran into a situation where a sister of a very dear friend of mine was killed, and I had this same horror reaction. My first impulse was to avoid her, but I didn't. I forced myself to face the situation with her. This may not sound like much to you, but the old me wouldn't have done this. As I say, I "noticed" with this girl—you see, it reached the point where I couldn't even talk. If someone in the family died, and my relatives wanted to talk about it, I tried to change the subject or to stop them. Now I know this wasn't good. And as I said, I wanted to go out and talk to this friend of mine and so I did—and we spent the whole afternoon talking about it, which she needed to do. And I found I wasn't disturbed at all—in fact, I felt so much better afterward that I even felt guilty about that (she laughs).

Pastor: That is, once you became involved with her in her suffering you "were taken out of yourself," as you put it before, and the experience was so novel and exhilarating that you were ashamed a bit for having such good feelings about it.

Mrs. Wenn: That's it exactly, but I just said to myself, "Why shouldn't you feel good about it, this is a real victory for you," and how satisfying to feel the warm embrace of my friend as she expressed her appreciation to me for coming. That's something I'll never forget.

Pastor: Means a great deal to you—

Mrs. Wenn: Now I know a little better what Jesus meant when he said, "If anyone would come after me, let him take up his cross and follow me" (pause). Oh, I still have to work at it, but I've really changed. When I first came to see you, I had the notion that you would make all of my troubles vanish and I wouldn't have any more problems (she laughs). I can't say that's happened. In fact, it's funny, but I got something different than what I came for. I guess I have just as many problems, but I am not overwhelmed by them like I was.

Mrs. Wenn is exhibiting how she is becoming aware of her transformation through the spontaneity of her compassion. She could serve a supportive role for her friend without suffering crippling paralysis from her fear of her own feelings. She was motivated to share her friend's burden without fear of being overwhelmed by it. She found she could suffer with her friend and, as a consequence, experience renewal rather than annihilation. She did not minimize either the extremity of the situation or the pain she felt in relation to it. Her suffering was real, but was more than compensated in the fulfillment she gained from being a source of strength and encouragement to her friend. Furthermore, she was no longer plagued with the nagging guilt that she was letting her friend down, and was happy with the courage of her action.

If the pastor has the skill to provoke the assimilation process and the patience to support it, he will greatly assist the person in moving through it. Ultimately, the pastor must understand and promote the assimilation of judgment through the total impact of his own relationship with God. Basic to this understanding is an appreciation of the "soul struggle" within man. J. Arthur Baird has set forth the nature of that struggle in a discussion of what he regards as Jesus' doctrine of man, as reflected in the Gospels:

Jesus' anthropology is given within the circle of crisis that characterizes his cosmology and epitomizes the very nature of God. He challenges man with the knowledge that he possesses the freedom and ability to receive the Kingdom, the power, the Spirit of God, and so to fill the God-shaped vacuum in his soul with a brand-new dimension of life, or else to reject God's presence of love and so to keep that soul on the psychosomatic level of death, dark and empty, subject to every demonic force of the flesh and the physical world. Jesus challenges man with a momentous choice between two soul conditions that are the human reflection of the love and the wrath of God. These he pictures in a series of crisis contrasts: between the spiritual and the physical man, between the man filled with light and the man of darkness, between the righteous and the sinner, the son of the Kingdom and the son of the evil one, between the man of life and the man who is still dead. There can be no neutrality. God's imperative is clear. Men are either one or the other; and by their choice do they judge themselves.[1]

The pastor's primary responsibility is to help the person bring the "crisis contrasts" within his own being into focus. Thus, he enables the person to take in both the negative and positive aspects of his own existence, consequently facilitating the assimilation of the judgments inherent in both. He may assume that persons who seek counseling are led by the Spirit, whether they are aware of it or not, toward life "on the level of the spirit" (Rom. 8:5 NEB). Therefore, the pastor who fulfills his function as counselor will *stay with* the person as he moves through the stages of the assimilation process, not pushing him, nor offering him illusory shortcuts, nor in any way depriving him of the freedom of facing the consequences of his own choices, but assuring him of the faithfulness and trust of a relationship within which he can face judgment and assimilate it.

The pastor's "staying with" the person should not be regarded as altogether passive. It involves confrontation; but confrontation is not pushing, either. Rather, the pastor puts himself in a position where the person must deal with him. He is involved. He is not simply letting the person "be," he is provoking him to "become."

[1] *The Justice of God in the Teachings of Jesus* (Philadelphia: Westminster Press, 1963), p. 198.

II Motivation and Variations

Lest the reader assume I am asserting that every person faithfully, methodically, and systematically marches through the previously outlined stages on his way to changed selfhood, or that it is always just a matter of going through stages in some kind of automatic process, I hasten to add several important words of disclaimer. Furthermore, I hope to add clarity to an understanding of the stages in the context of the total dynamics of personal change and transformation.

Two important words of qualification to the interpretation of the stages are required at this point The first has to do with what must happen prior to the first stage of the assimilation process. Thus, what I will say in that regard may be summed up under the word *motivation*. How does the person get to the point of acknowledging the "over-againstness" of judgment in the first place? What sensitivity is already presupposed at the first stage?

The second word refers to individual modes of appropriating judgment and of responding to its demands upon the person. The term *variations* perhaps best conveys what is meant here. Once a person moves into a subsequent stage, does he ever revert to a former stage? If he has attained the sixth stage, may he slip to the first? If such reversals do occur, what do they imply for the whole process of the assimilation of judgment?

We may surely assume that the person who undertakes

to involve himself in the disciplined, often painful, task of assimilating judgment—in commonsense terms, "growing" —is motivated. We may also undoubtedly assume that if he is not motivated, he will not undergo the struggle which such learning requires. Abraham Maslow notes both "deficiency" and "growth" motivation, saying the former arises from "basic or instinctoid needs," and the latter from "trends to self-actualization," and an "unceasing trend toward unity, integration, or synergy." [1] For the purpose of making an arbitrary alignment to illustrate my concern, I see my stages as falling generally within the category of "growth and motivation." I affirm, with Maslow, "basic needs and self-actualization do not contradict each other any more than do childhood and maturity. One passes into the other and is a necessary prerequisite for it." [2] This is precisely the assumption I make in regard to the stages, acknowledging that meeting deficiency motivation precedes them.

The process of the assimilation of judgment in pastoral counseling is predicated on the assumption that the person is already motivated to encounter judgment. This means that something has happened to bring him to the first stage, wherein he is sensitized to judgment. In his classic book *Pastoral Counseling*, Seward Hiltner sees the first assumption regarding pastoral counseling as: "The parishioner senses something is wrong, and at least in a measure that the difficulty may be seen within himself." [3] Obviously that statement implies that the person has already reached a point of readiness for counseling to take place. In a sense,

---

[1] *Toward a Psychology of Being* (Princeton: D. Van Nostrand Co., 1962), p. 23.
[2] *Ibid.*, p. 24.
[3] *Pastoral Counseling* (Nashville: Abingdon Press, 1949), p. 20.

the beginning of therapy is presupposed. The person may not be conscious of the whole measure of his concern, but he has a degree of awareness of his responsibility for what has and is happening.

Considerable "pre-counseling" work, as Hiltner has termed it, may be required before the person is prepared to begin the assimilation process which takes place within the counseling relationship itself. The pre-counseling task of the pastor is to offer judgment as "love at the right time," as I discussed it previously, which means, in part, to confront the person where he is in acceptance and in faith in the person's capacity to move responsibly from where he is to where he may be in constructive attitudes and actions.

Growth motivation is the positive outcome of the assimilation of judgment. The growth-motivated person is in the process of finding how to learn from his experiences. In relation to the externalizing-internalizing process, which I mentioned earlier, he has learned to internalize. He is thus freed to act appropriately, decisively, and effectively. In other words, he shoulders responsibility. He sees what needs to be done and imaginatively puts himself into the task.

The determinants which govern (self-actualizing people) are now primarily inner ones, rather than social or environmental. They are the laws of their own inner nature, their potentialities and capacities, their talents, their latent resources, their creative impulses, their needs to know themselves and to become more and more integrated and unified, more and more aware of what they really are, of what they really want, of what their call or vocation or fate is to be.[4]

[4] *Ibid.*, p. 32.

As his deficiency needs are met, the person is freed to become growth-motivated person. Hence the meeting of "deficit" needs is a prior order of business.

His anxious dependence on his environment breeds hostility. Until he can trust his environment, growth motivation eludes him. The hope for breaking down the walls of hostility comes through his encounter of the love and acceptance of the significant other person. With such support, he learns not to fear but to welcome judgment which opens up his growth motivation, makes him more discerning, more trusting of his capacity to judge, and open to further judgment. He is thus not overwhelmed by judgment, because he has the ego strength to incorporate it, adding to his own wisdom and stature.

A certain ego strength is already presupposed. Obviously, not everyone who seeks counseling has sufficient gratification of deficit needs to move to the level of meeting growth needs.

To push the problem of deficiency motivation deeper, the person with a lack of personal or social conscience, or in a psychosis of greater or lesser intensity, is probably quite remote from the first stage in the assimilation of judgment. Hence, he requires patient, persistent, discerning psychiatric assistance in getting to that point. The severely depressed person, for example, is not a candidate for the antithetical (first) stage because he usually lacks sufficient ego strength to hold up his side of the antithesis. The competition is one-sided. The countering judgment is the winner by default; hence no assimilation is possible.

In more technical terms, Karl Menninger's categorization of "five orders of dysfunction" is highly suggestive of what must be dealt with prior to the first stage of the assimilation process. The first two orders probably represent levels wherein the assimilation of judgment may be regarded as possible. The first order of dyscontrol, commonly called "nervousness," is a slight disturbance of organization and of coping. "Habitual coping devices can be taken off guard anywhere, any time." [5] Increased tension and often increased repression occur. "Usually states of First Order dyscontrol represent a transitional or quickly reversible phase." [6] In most cases when the stress factors in the face of which the symptoms are created disappear, the person "feels all right" and is "getting along."

A second order of dyscontol "is a slight but definite detachment of the person from his environment, and—simultaneously—from his loyalty to reality." [7] This includes what may be regarded as the neuroses—hysterical and obsessional behaviors, etc.—compensatory and tension-reducing devices which are at once painful to the person and his environment.

The third order of dyscontrol is characterized by the escape of the "dangerous, destructive impulses," which is "a manifestation of acute or chronic ego failure." [8] These destructive impulses are outbursts, attacks, assaults, and social offenses which are evidences of the loss of the "ego's efforts to restrain and control dangerous impulses."

The extremes of what Menninger terms personality "dysorganization" are seen in the fourth and fifth orders of dyscontrol. In the fourth order loyalty to reality is either largely or completely abandoned. It is

"represented by those extreme states of dysorganization, regression, and reality repudiation which constitute the classical

[5] *The Vital Balance* (New York: Viking Press, 1963), p. 163.
[6] *Ibid.*, p. 173.
[7] *Ibid.*, p. 174.
[8] *Ibid.*, p. 248.

picture of severe mental illness—so-called psychoses. . . . They represent a penultimate effort to avoid something worse, viz., Fifth Order dysorganization—malignant anxiety and depression eventuating in death, often by suicide." [9]

The "orders of dysfunction" are barriers to the assimilation of judgment; in fact, they are actually abortive ways of reacting to what judgment is about. If, as in the case especially of the three latter orders of dyscontrol, anxiety is not functioning constructively toward a creative, integrative thrust, the person is not likely to be motivated toward the assimilation of judgment. To put the matter positively, the assimilation of judgment is part of the fusing and integrating process which must already be set in motion if assimilation is to occur. Clearly, reinforcement of the ego is essential to the process. It is the ego which assimilates the judgment.

Having noted levels of dyscontrol which may be regarded as barriers to incorporating judgment, we now need to face the question: What is the point at which the person is ready to begin the assimilation process? How do we discern when the person is entering into the stages? Although assigning a point in time when the antithetical stage actually begins is exceedingly difficult, a general designation may be given. When the person begins to "internalize" in the sense of engaging the ego with what judgment is about, he is probably moving into the first stage. He now sees the "I" as responsible, in some measure, for what the judgment implies. He is not denying, evading, rationalizing, or using other dodging methods, but is "facing up" to the judgment, despite the fact that he has not yet begun to appropriate its meaning for him.

[9] *Ibid.*, p. 250.

An illustration of the critical point in the preassimilation process is seen in the case of Mrs. Kinn. She anxiously nurtured, yet vowed she hated, dependence upon her husband. Early in her marriage, she said, she had invested him with a halo. "But that sure has become tarnished!" she added in a tone of disgust. She accused him of becoming involved in an extramarital "love game with one of my supposedly best friends," as she put it.

The three of us, Mrs. Kinn, her husband, and I, met in a subsequent marital counseling session. He sought to minimize his relationship with the other woman, a tactic which infuriated Mrs. Kinn. He said the so-called affair had been more than two years in the past, but his wife was so "hooked" on the subject she was driving him "nuts." "I'm with her, ain't I?" he protested, gesturing toward Mrs. Kinn. "That oughta say somethin' about where my real interests are. I've said I'm sorry about whatever I may've done wrong a hundred times, but that just ain't enough for her."

"What gets me is the way he lies about what actually happened," she countered. "In fact, that's just it. It isn't so much that he went out with her. He can have her if he wants her. It's that he won't tell me the truth about it."

"You don't really trust him, I gather," I said.

"Well, everybody has said I'm a fool to believe him, because I was the last one to know what was going on. You know, a wife is always the last one to know," she said, biting her lip.

"Makes you feel pretty foolish," I responded.

"You aren't kiddin.' He enjoys seeing me squirm." Her eyes flashed in anger as she looked at him quickly, then turned her head away from him.

They exchanged heated retorts for a few moments. Suddenly he cautiously but firmly put his hand on hers. The tension eased and the interview closed on a quiet note of temporary truce.

Mrs. Kinn telephoned me a few days prior to the next scheduled interview. She said she was not functioning well, "not doing anything but moping around," and wondered how long she could "go on this way." I perceived she was in a rather serious depressed state and referred her to one of the psychiatrists in the city. She was hospitalized for a time, and I did not hear from her for several months. Her psychiatrist, with whom I have worked closely for some time, referred her back to me for resumption of counseling.

"*I* have been too dependent on my husband," she said in the early part of the interview. "*I* see now that *I* have been really smothering him. *I* have been holding on to him too much. *I* know now, *I* must let go. He is an open, friendly person. It's funny, but that bothers me. (Judgment acknowledged.) I'm not friendly with people like he is. Oh, I have good friends. But he makes me mad, sometimes, the way he attracts people—especially women." She paused, then continued in a musing mode. "I wonder what that says about me."

Her first encounter with the implied judgment in her husband's responsiveness to other people was evident in the interview following her treatment. She was beginning at this point to *discern the nature of the judgment* and, to a degree, her responsibility in relation to it. Quite properly, in the subsequent marital counseling, he was to become as implicated in the assimilation process as she was. Thus, their communication with each other and acceptance of each other began to improve.

Leaps and Reversals in the Stages

Not only must we recognize what must occur dynamically in preparation for the assimilation process, but also we must see what actually happens in the person's working through the stages themselves.

First, I should say precisely what the stages are and are not. They are clues to the reintegrating struggle going on within the person. As categories they are useful in ways similar to those described by Karl Menninger in his explication of orders of dysfunction. The various orders of dyscontrol which we have described and illustrated are not pigeonholes into which people may be fitted; they are only still photographs of a moving picture of human life.

Likewise, my descriptions of stages may be regarded as still shots of people in the process of assimilating judgment. If these could be shown in their actual dramatic sequences and in the light of the highly individual variations surrounding them in the real theater of life, a more accurate reporting of their true dynamics could be given. However, such effort would require a whole set of works, necessarily compiled from meticulous, painstaking observations of data over an extended period of time, a task hardly within the scope of one volume.

Hence, I have but given glimpses of phenomena in which I have detected certain observable checkpoints. These have recurred with sufficient frequency and in such strength as insistently to lay claim on my attention, but they are in nowise to be construed as depicting necessary or irreversible steps in any kind of deterministic sense. In fact, the assimilation of judgment takes place in a total context of personality dynamics which actually eventuates as a series of leaps and reversals. Thus, a person may bypass

130

one or more stages, or in the same manner he may revert to a previous stage.

There are numerous variations in dynamics of the assimilation process, depending upon shifts in internal and external forces working within or upon the person. The process is deeply affected by what Karl Menninger describes as a struggle for "compromise."

Life is thus a succession of more or less wide swings in the disturbance of equilibrium of internal and external systems which must be brought into an ecological balance that is inevitably a fleeting, dynamic, and unstable one—Bertalanffy's steady state. The vital balance is thus a perpetually unstable restabilizing.[10]

Disturbances in the "ecological balance" in the organism's relationship to its environment supply the motive power for the refinement of judgment. Thus, the intensity of motivation toward the assimilation of judgment is influenced by the degrees of the swings in the disturbances of equilibrium. Obviously, this dynamic evokes myriads of variations among persons and within persons, in moving through stages in the assimilation of judgment, depending upon how the ego is affected by these internal and external forces.

A notable and classical biblical example of a leap in the assimilation of judgment is seen in the conversion of the apostle Paul. The release of creative potential comes on with such obvious and dramatic force that, in the centuries which have felt his pervasive influence upon thought and behavior, many persons have regarded his experience as the norm for conversion. One negative consequence has

[10] *Ibid.*, p. 114.

been that some have assumed Paul's type of conversion was the only valid one.

The antithetical stage is clearly implied in the narrative regarding Paul's conversion in the book of Acts; "But Saul, still breathing threats and murder against the disciples of the Lord, went to the high priest and asked him for letters to the synagogues at Damascus, so that if he found any belonging to the Way, men or women, he might bring them bound to Jerusalem." (Acts 9:1-2.) Paul's attitude was reflected in the words of the voice of which he was conscious during the episode, "Saul, Saul, why do you persecute me?" He was encountering judgment in the image of Jesus Christ. This judgment was alien to him ("who are you, Lord?"), undifferentiated ("when his eyes were opened, he could see nothing"), and unassimilated ("for three days he was without sight, and neither ate nor drank").

Nevertheless, the reality of the judgment had burst upon him, he experienced forgiveness at the hands of those who ministered to him, and his transformation began to take place ("and immediately something like scales fell from his eyes and he regained his sight"). Although not germane to the particular point under discussion, the forgiveness mediated through Ananias was the truly enabling act toward effecting the transformation.

Thus for Paul, as for many, the intervening stages are passed over. Despite this fact, the remarkable coincidence between Paul's observations in letters attributed to him and my reflections upon clinical data originally prompted me to be aware of the existence of stages.[11]

Surely he was aware of something like these stages in

---

[11] I have cited the sources from Paul's letters throughout the previous discussions on judgment. Therefore, I will not reiterate the quotations.

the earlier phases of his own development. By the time of his conversion, a peculiar combination of internal and external forces resulted in the *kairos* in terms of which his leap was precipitated.

A modern example of bypassing stages, in what I am terming the "leap," may give contemporaneity to the point I am making about one kind of variation on our theme. Mrs. Drenn, in her late thirties, is married, the mother of three children, and is a professional musician. She desired to talk with her pastor, she said, "to see if I can do something about my religious illiteracy." Although she said the latter jokingly, she was soon giving clear evidence of being quite resistant to the pastor and on the defensive with him.

Finally he said, "I am getting a very uneasy feeling—as though I am walking a tightrope with you, and you are watching me very critically to see that I don't make a misstep."

She looked at him intently for a moment. Then, with a deep sigh, she dropped her eyes and toyed anxiously with the ridge of upholstery on the arm of her chair. "Yeah," she said with increased tone in her voice, "I really do walk a tightrope with most everybody, including myself. I am so driven to succeed that I don't even see other people. I am really properly called a prima donna, I guess, but I don't want to alienate everybody like I've been doing."

Within a few days after this interview, Mrs. Drenn's father, whom she had said she detested throughout her life, came to visit her, saying that his wife, Mrs. Drenn's mother, had filed for divorce and had kicked him out. Although she said she could not yet revise her feelings toward him, she was able to treat him differently than she had ever done. She confessed she was surprised at his sincere expression of gratitude, "a quality in him I never dreamed possible." Her changed self-concept was pervading all her relationships, she said, and she was "having fun discovering people, despite some painful discoveries, too, about myself."

Obviously much critical material has been deleted from this illustration, leaving it sounding naïvely like a fairy tale. However, the real points are: Mrs. Drenn did actually make the leap into the stage of transformation, and this was undoubtedly precipitated by a number of internal and external forces coming to focus fortuitously at critical points in her encounter with her pastor and her father.

Reversals are discouraging to the person and disappointing to the pastor but are realistic eventualities within the pastoral counseling relationship. They reflect instances in which internal and external forces interact to increase tension in the face of a newly posed threat. Thus, judgment in a different form is confronted, and the person is thrown back to an earlier stage.

One case portrays a painful reversal for a young woman, Miss Dopp, who was a teacher in one of the elementary schools in her city. She had begun her counseling with the recognition that she despised people whom she regarded as intellectually and culturally inferior to her. Her "perfectionism," as she confessed it, had led her to make such heavy demands upon herself that she could not tolerate her own burden. She also thought "it would be nice" to be able to accept the parents and other teachers with whom she worked, because she felt so isolated she was miserable. She said she assumed she was unmarried largely because "I don't think any man can measure up to what I expect."

In a relatively brief time of counseling with her pastor,

she began to find great satisfaction in improved relationships with her peers and with other people generally. She began dating regularly and finally became interested particularly in a fellow male teacher who seemed to return her regard.

She had moved to the stage of conceptualization (sixth) of her expanding self-concept, and was apparently experiencing some transformation, when a sudden shock sent her into a spin. The announcement of the man's engagement to a girl in another city "really flipped" her, as she put it. She immediately reverted to the first stage, pondering the question of how her perfectionism may have crept in to drive him away. She found herself looking down on people again and struggling with her old thoughts. Judgment had become antithetical to her again.

However, she found that her reversal was not long-lived. Neither was she as threatened by it as she first feared. "I guess now that I know how far I have come," she said to the pastor. "I know what is possible, and I don't fear 'slipping' as much as I thought I would. Oh, of course, this has been a real blow to me, but it didn't take me as long to get out of the doldrums as it used to. Not only that, but during the past few months I have developed a new way of relating to people that's shown me what's possible. I don't think I can ever forget that! I just seem to be bouncing back quicker, that's all. Of course, I love teaching, and that's helped. But—ah—several of the parents came in this week to tell me how much they appreciate what I am doing—now that's a switch! (She laughs.) I mean—ah—it wasn't that way last year! But, you can see, I'm doing better. I know I've been pretty low, the last few weeks, and—it's been good to have you to talk to."

As Miss Dopp has shown, reversals do occur, but usually they do not represent major setbacks. Movement through the stages appears to facilitate the process. Reversion to a previous stage may take place a number of times involving the same data of judgment. Of course, assimilating new data requires repetition of the process; however, each experience of moving through stages increases a person's faith in his ability to do so and therefore gives him confidence and hope in the face of each new datum of judgment.

Patterns of getting to and moving through the process of the assimilation of judgment vary from person to person and from time to time. The variances may be attributed to differences in stress factors resulting from peculiar combinations of external and internal forces. Although a pastor or other helping person will be able to reinforce the process, he cannot and should not attempt to control it.

Despite diversities in modes of responding to judgment and differences in the capacity to consolidate gains made in moving through stages, the process of assimilating judgment by incorporating it in stages seems to be evident. Considerable supportive effort on the part of caring and concerned people is required if the person is to initiate and complete the process. Realizing this fact, in the subsequent chapters I will concentrate especially upon the pastoral context, to show how the pastor and the church may effect and sustain the person's assimilation process.

PART III

12   The Pastor
and the
Assimilation Process

In his precounseling and counseling work with individuals and groups the pastor is properly both *facilitator*
and *confronter*. As facilitator, he enables the person to
undertake and complete his own assimilation of judgment;
as confronter he also allows and prompts the person to do
so. In the latter case, the pastor becomes the significant
other in relation to whom the person can check his own
views. Both facilitation and confrontation must be viewed
carefully to prevent misinterpretation of what is implied in
each action. I will devote this entire chapter to a discussion
of my intended meaning of the terms as they apply to the
pastor's counseling function.

The Pastor as Facilitator

As counselor, the pastor properly supports and reinforces
the person's integrating tendencies. He has faith in the
capacity of the person to assimilate judgment and facilitates
the process. He does this by offering himself to a relationship with persons or groups in which persons are free to
engage in self-exploration. Thus, he becomes an enabler of
the assimilation process. Enablement is a skill which can be
learned, but it is also an attitude which comes out of the
pastor's basic orientation toward life. We can talk about the

facilitating action of the pastor in terms of conditions, but we must also regard it as having the character of the unconditional.

Facilitative conditions are rather commonly regarded as empathy, positive regard, genuineness, concreteness, and self-disclosure. So much has been said and written about *empathy* that it seems tiringly redundant to rehash it here. However, as an educator and clinician, I am aware that a review of a concept from another look at its various facets is rarely out of order. To restate the technical understanding of the word: empathy is "the imaginative projective of one's own psychological behavior into an object, event, or other person; the ability to identify intelligently with the problems and difficulties of another person." [1] Empathy is the condition in which one is participating in the personal structuring of the other—his ideas, feelings, etc. Such participation is not to the point of the loss of one's own identity, but is the opposite of calloused avoidance of the other's feelings. Carl Rogers has defined empathy:

The state of empathy, or being empathic, is to perceive the internal frame of reference of another with accuracy and with the emotional components which pertain thereto, as if one were the other person, but without ever losing the "as if" condition. Thus it means to sense the hurt or the pleasure of another as he senses it, and to perceive the causes thereof as he perceives them, but without ever losing the recognition that it is *as if* I was hurt, or pleased, etc. If this "as if" quality is lost, then, the state is identification. [2]

---

[1] Philip L. Harriman, *Handbook of Psychological Terms* (Princeton: Littlefield, Adams & Co., 1959), p. 52.

[2] An unpublished paper entitled "A Theory of Therapy, Personality, and Interpersonal Relationship as Developed in the Client-Centered Framework," p. 26.

A minister friend of mine was once prompted by his reading of Ezekiel 3:15 to preach a sermon entitled "And I Sat Where They Sat." The text is: "Then I came to them of the captivity at Telabib, that dwelt by the river of Chebar, and I sat where they sat, and remained there astonished among them seven days" (KJV).

His preparation for the sermon included his actually going into the sanctuary, sitting quietly in one of the pews, and asking himself the soul-searching question: "What do I need to hear from that pulpit there that will speak to my condition?" "This was no idle pious exercise or melodramatic gimmick," he related to me. "I meant business! I felt it. I waited and listened expectantly as I felt my people must do. I actually wept a little as I thought of the many times I had fed them stones when they asked for bread, and I smiled, and felt warm, when I thought of the times when I had felt the gratitude when, as I saw them reaching toward me, I had filled their hearts with 'gifts of great measure.' I preached the sermon the following Sunday," my friend continued. "Afterward, one of my parishioners shook my hand and said softly, 'Thank you, pastor, you touched me deeply. Your sermon came at precisely the right time for me. It's given me a great deal to think about.' "

The minister's imaginative act of sitting where the other sits is an essential condition of a helpful relationship. He may not communicate his empathy in so many words, but his imaginative effort is communicated to the person and is usually received by him appreciatively. Of course, there are exceptions to the latter assertion, especially in the case of the person who does not trust any kind of communication. Nevertheless, the continual offering of empathy extends the hope of the person's eventual overcoming of his mistrust.

Positive regard is also a facilitative or enabling condition of a counseling relationship. Positive regard is a basic valuing of the other person—and meeting him with attitudes of warmth, caring, liking, interest, and respect. If my perception of some self-experience in another makes a positive difference in my awareness, then I am experiencing positive regard for that person.

An indication of one person's awareness of her counselor's positive regard is given in the following excerpt from an interview with a thirty-four-year-old woman, Mrs. Tremm. I had previously counseled with her over a period of several months. She had been "deeply hurt and disappointed" by her husband, who she discovered was involved in an extramarital affair with her "so-called best friend." The other woman's death from cancer had terminated the relationship. Mrs. Tremm had discontinued regularly scheduled appointments, because, as she put it, "I am beginning to get to the place where I can live with it."

The following interview took place approximately five months later. She had called asking to see me as soon as possible. I arranged an appointment for her to accommodate her travel schedule en route home from her work. As soon as she arrived in my office, she slumped into the chair rather dejectedly and said:

Mrs. Tremm: Well, I'm back again. Sometimes I just feel like ending it all and getting it all done with.

Mr. Colston: You get terribly discouraged about keeping up the struggle, I guess.

Mrs. Tremm: Yes, I do, and I know I shouldn't feel this way. But despite my efforts to tell myself differently, I do.

142

Mr. Colston: No amount of pep talking to yourself keeps you from getting down on yourself, I gather.

Mrs. Tremm: That's right. I know it's wrong to have these feelings—you're just not supposed to get mad.

Mr. Colston: Who said?

Mrs. Tremm: Well, everybody, but—I don't know—lots of people (she waves her arms).

Mr. Colston: Well, what do you do then when you feel somebody is being unfair to you?

Mrs. Tremm: (She swings her arms dramatically in a wide arc.) I just blow up all over the place! (She pauses. Her shoulders slump. She looks down and drums repeatedly with her fingers on the table.) No I don't. I just tell myself, "Now don't get mad." Then finally I can't hold it anymore, then I *do* blow up all over the place. (She continues on this theme for about fifteen minutes. Then she speaks dejectedly.) I have just come to the conclusion that nobody cares.

Mr. Colston: Not even me. You don't feel that I care?

Mrs. Tremm: I don't know. Oh, I suppose you do a little. If I were to go home and blow my brains out, you'd probably come to my funeral. But beyond that, I don't really know—

Mr. Colston: I'll tell you this—if I learn that you are trying to commit suicide, I'll do anything in my power to stop you!

Mrs. Tremm: You will?

Mr. Colston: Yes, Ma'am!

Mrs. Tremm: Because you don't believe in suicide?

Mr. Colston: Because I believe in you!

Mrs. Tremm was apparently reassured of my positive regard and could accept the close of the interview without "hanging on" as I had experienced in previous sessions. She had said to me earlier in the interview that she had been at the point of calling me to help her get hospitalization again (she has had several periods of psychiatric treatment), but, she said, "I didn't want to give in. I wanted to keep going." She said she didn't know why she called me, except that I understood her better than anyone she knew. She said she felt better when she talked with me because I seemed to take an interest in her. She was responding to positive regard.

A person is *genuine* in a particular respect when his experience in this area coincides with a correspondence in awareness, and his awareness is exemplified in appropriate expression. If the person is experiencing fear (or anger, or tenderness, etc.), is aware of this experiencing, and is free to express it when appropriate, then he is genuine.

Lack of genuineness is either to deny feelings to awareness or to be aware of such feelings but not express them when appropriate. The presence of such feelings, which may be communicated in nonverbal symbols, may be quite obvious to the other person, who sees the discrepancy between what is said and what is being communicated. This may shake the trust of the other person, who may already be in doubt regarding the acceptability of some of his feelings.

Pastor Hartt's third interview with a young woman, Mrs. Bonn, was a critical session in their counseling relationship. Previously she had told the pastor she had been seeing the husband of one of her friends, that she was in love with him, and wished to obtain a divorce in order to marry him. During the subsequent weeks the pastor had been sought out by each of the other three people involved: Mrs. Bonn's husband, her lover, Mr. Grib, and his wife. Mr. Grib had discontinued his relationship with Mrs. Bonn. He also had not called and had refused to accept her calls. Mrs. Bonn interpreted his action as temporary rejection to pacify his wife, who she said "is an expert at creating scenes." She refused to believe he did not wish to see her.

The pastor noticed she was being rather evasive and restive throughout the session. Finally she said:

Mrs. Bonn: You talked to Sid (Mr. Grib) last night, didn't you?

Pastor: Yes, I did.

Mrs. Bonn: I finally got word through to him and suggested he come and see you. He called me, and that's the first time in a month, and he told me he'd try to make it last night.

Pastor: Well, he did come.

Mrs. Bonn: Did he say anything that I should know about?

Pastor: I can't tell what he said, because that would be violating my own rule about keeping information confidential. I will keep what he says in confidence just as I intend to keep what you say in trust.

Mrs. Bonn: Oh, but I don't care what you tell him about what I say to you.

Pastor: (His face flushes a bit.) But he didn't give me that option.

Mrs. Bonn: Then I don't see the use in my coming here for counseling. You are the only contact I have with him. I have no way of knowing what's going on, or how he feels.

Pastor: You've got to be kidding!

Mrs. Bonn: What?

Pastor: As I see it, you are saying quite bluntly that you want to use me. If my only function is to be a communication line between you and Mr. Grib, I'll have to agree with you that my usefulness is over. I just can't do that.

Mrs. Bonn: (She looks down briefly; then looks at the pastor again.) I am afraid I am putting it rather badly. I am sorry. Seeing you is really helping me. I don't want to make you angry with me. Maybe these are some things I need to talk about. May I see you again?

Pastor: Yes, indeed. Is next Tuesday at 7 P.M. ok?

The pastor did not scold, shame, or denigrate Mrs. Bonn. He was aware of his own anger at her attempts to manipulate him and he was expressing his feelings in an appropriate response. He did not berate her, even by implication, for perceiving him as a push-over. Instead, he was as much amused as offended by her efforts, and responded with humor to her threats to quit the counseling. Nevertheless, he made clear his perception of what she was doing and his feeling about it. Thus, he was being genuine in his relationship with her. She valued this and let him know by stating her deep concern that she be permitted to continue in counseling with him.

Concreteness is the actual embodiment of an event. An event is a unique happening which has never taken place in quite this way before, and will never occur again in precisely the same manner. The conditions which occasion an event are peculiar to it. Thus, the event is novel and particular. An event happens as various energies meet. The coalescence is concretion. The opposite of concretion is abstraction, which is the act of moving away from the event in generalization. To abstract is to draw inferences from the concrete, thus to theorize about it.

In simple terms, concreteness in counseling is the condition of being there—being present—concentrating one's energies on the actual encounter. To generalize is to impose an abstraction which has been drawn from a previous event. Applied to counseling, this means the counselor may be off somewhere in abstraction, not really engaging the other in this moment of his experiencing. What is triggered off in the counselor may be somewhat unrelated to the total

146

experiencing of the counselee. The person experiences the abstractions as cues that the counselor is not with him. Although he may feel frustrated and isolated, he usually does not give up hope, but offers the counselor repeated opportunities to make contact with him. He persists precisely because he wishes to overcome his isolation and to be understood. Fortunately for both the counselor and himself, if he gets glimpses of understanding, he is encouraged and will maintain his efforts. However, if he tries repeatedly without success, he will eventually give up this struggle as futile.

The pastor's communication of his concreteness is not merely in verbal but also in nonverbal symbols. Hence concreteness presupposes the conditions of empathy, positive regard, and genuineness. The counselee will tolerate a degree of abstractness if these conditions are present, but usually will not endure a predominance of generalizations, despite his appreciation of the pastor as a "nice fella." The pastor's abstractions may alienate the person by leaving him feeling cut off, left out, or woefully ignorant. Since the magic words seem to him esoteric and remote, he may react in anger or disappointment.

The pastor who is relevant in counseling is really listening and interacting with the person. He is not absent in abstraction, but there in his concreteness. He is aware of his own and the other's present experiencing.

An illustration of abstraction is shown in the following brief part of a pastor's interview with a couple who were on the verge of divorce. The couple, both in their late twenties, were parents of a two-year-old child.

Mrs. Wann: I have had about all I can stand! Tom is out every night. I don't know who with. He never says anything when

147

he comes home. But he spends all his money, so he must be having himself a time.

Mr. Wann: Well, see, she's always nagging me and I get kinda tired of it and, see, me and the boys get together for a little cards once in a while.

Mrs. Wann: Once in a while? Every night, practically!

Mr. Wann: No, it ain't. I'm workin' part of the time.

Pastor: You are doing some gambling?

Mr. Wann: I wouldn't call it that, just a few bucks now and then.

Pastor: But you are gambling.

Mrs. Wann: Isn't that awful—him lying like that?

Pastor: Well, we all make mistakes once in a while. Remember God is a forgiving God. Tom, you should commit yourself to Christ and start from there. Why don't you come to the church night dinner next Wednesday night?

Mr. Wann: I don't know—ah—I may have to work at night next week.

Mrs. Wann: Oh, Tom, you know you won't have to work next Wednesday night.

Pastor: I would like to tell you both something here. It seems to me the problem of all of us is self-control. You are both giving in to your feelings, and that causes friction.

Mr. Wann: Yeah, well maybe so, I'll try to do that, pastor. Oh—thanks very much for your time.

In addition to being rather insensitive to the dynamics of the relationship between Tom and Mary Wann, the pastor was continually moving away from them in his generalized responses. He was listening for opportunities to teach them but was failing to hear them. Although he was aware of Tom's "innocence" game as far as his gambling pattern was concerned, he was not responding to Tom's feelings toward Mary. Likewise, he was encountering Mary only by implication, suggesting she needed to control herself and her vindictiveness. The potential group (the couple and the pastor) had met but not really come together. There was no coalescence—no concretion—because the pastor himself did not represent concreteness.

Self-disclosure is an act of revealing oneself to another. The self is a mystery which is both hidden and revealed. To reveal oneself is to take the risk of being hurt by a broken trust or betrayed by a careless, cunning, or spiteful "friend." Nevertheless, relationships are formed out of the open, honest disclosure of each to the other. The common bond of mutual faith and trust where it is held in integrity is the true pathway to wholeness.

Dr. Sidney S. Jourard, in a book entitled *The Transparent Self: Openness, Effectiveness, and Health,* has said:

Self-disclosure, letting another person know what you think, feel, or want is the most direct means (though not the only means) by which an individual can make himself known to another person.[3]

Would it be too arbitrary an assumption to propose that people become clients *because they do not disclose themselves in some optimal degree to the people in their life?* [4] And it seems to be another empirical fact *that no man can acknowledge his real self to himself (that is, know himself) except as an outcome of disclosing himself to another person.*[5]

I have gradually come to see therapy not as a setting in which one person, the therapist, *does things to a patient . . .* but rather as a relationship . . . in which growth of *both* parties is an outcome.[6]

[3] *The Transparent Self: Openness, Effectiveness, and Health* (Princeton: D. Van Nostrand, 1964), p. 24.

[4] *Ibid.,* p. 21.

[5] *Ibid.,* p. 5.

[6] *Ibid.,* p. 67. I have been using the latter phrase for some time; naturally, therefore, I concur with his view.

The illustration given below shows how the self-disclosure of co-leaders of a group of ministers affected one of the members of the group. He had previously resigned his church and became engaged in another line of work. However, since he had committed himself to join the group, he continued to meet with them. Later, while still associated with the group, he returned to the parish with renewed interest and a growing sense of fulfillment. He reported that his decision had been greatly influenced by the session in which he first began to see the two leaders as human beings. I will call the minister Matt. The other group members involved in this interchange were Peter, Gray, and Art. The excerpt is as follows:

Peter: Matt, you are bugging me.

Matt: (Looks surprised.) Why?

Peter: You give me the feeling that you don't regard yourself as being in the same league with me. You strike me as a picture of the old alum that's come back on his fifth anniversary to give the underclassmen the lowdown.

Matt: What do you mean?

Peter: I see you over there just jabbing away at each one of us.

Gray: Yeah, I have been getting the "brunt" of it a few times, and I have been pretty angry with you.

Matt: (Nonchalantly) You didn't show it!

Gray: I kept feeling sorry for you, because I thought you were bitter about the pastorate. I thought I'd probably get to like you, if I learned to know you, now I'm not so sure. (Matt laughs along with other members of the group.)

Art: (He speaks to Gray.) I have felt he was trying to convince himself. (He turns to Matt.) You seem especially out to pick on Peter, Gray, and me.

(This interchange among the four continued for several minutes. Then:)

Matt: You guys have spotted something in me that I didn't

150

realize was there. I have some pretty strong feelings about your being parish pastors.

Leader A: You have some unresolved conflicts about the parish?

Matt: Apparently. I'm just now realizing it. I thought I was quite happy with my decision to leave it. But, I have noticed too, how I seem to be fighting it, and it comes out here in this group especially. Jay (he addresses leader B), you have brought out some feelings which made me think you have struggled with this.

Leader B: I think I said I had once decided to transfer into another field where counseling was the main focus, but the more I became involved, the more I was forced to come to terms with my basic theological interest. Finally, I found I was moving back into the ministry.

Matt: (He laughs) Maybe I'm trying to fight myself back into the parish.

Considerable discussion followed in which both leaders revealed themselves to the group.

At the termination session Art made the following comment: "I had always believed if the counselor or group leader revealed much of himself, he would lose the respect of members of the group. However, my experience here has been just the opposite. I have felt closer to our two group leaders, and I must say respected them more rather than less, as I began to appreciate their genuineness. It seemed to me their authority increased, but I was becoming less conscious of it as authority. They accepted and respected our taking turns at being the group leaders. I appreciated that."

Thomas C. Oden presents a hypothesis growing out of his dialogue with Jourard's material, which corresponds with my view of what is basic to the assimilation process.

He says: *"An adequate theory of therapy must not only understand therapeutic growth as a product of human self-disclosure, but authentic human self-disclosure as a response to the self-disclosure of God in being itself."* [7]

Oden states the central thesis of Christian theology as "the will of God to make himself known is the will of One who loves, and therefore loves to be known as One who loves." [8] The divine self-disclosure, he asserts, provides the conditions for full and free human self-disclosure. Gratitude for the gift of the divine self-disclosure overflows in the act of human self-disclosure.

The Pastor as Confronter

The pastor's confrontation of the person may promote the process of assimilation of judgment in that person. However, this is likely to occur only if the facilitating conditions are already present. In an empirical study of the effects of the counselor's confrontation of the person in counseling, Susan C. Anderson, of the University of Massachusetts, found that when it was accompanied by "facilitative conditions" (empathy, positive regard, genuineness, concreteness, and self-disclosure), *confrontation tended to increase the person's self-exploration.* When these conditions were at a low level in the counselor's approach, *confrontation was never followed by increased self-exploration.* Confrontation was defined in the study as "the therapist's pointing out a discrepancy between his own and the client's way of viewing a situation." [9]

[7] *Kerygma and Counseling* (Philadelphia: Westminster Press, 1966), p. 43.

[8] *Ibid.*, p. 45.

[9] "Effects of Confrontation by High- and Low-Functioning Therapists," J. *Counseling Psychology,* XV (1968), 411.

The author distinguished several ways in which confrontation was said to occur:

(1) The counselor points out the discrepancy between what the person wishes to be (his ideal self) and what he is (his actual self). For example:

Man, aged thirty-six: I wear the pants in our family. I've had a thing about this for a long time. I think the man should exert his authority and be the head of the house.

Pastor: I wonder if you really feel you are. You have been making such a point of it the last few moments.

(2) The person "expresses an increased awareness of himself as if this were the magical solution to all his problems."

Man, age twenty-seven: I have changed a lot since my wife and I were separated. I've learned a great deal. (He turns toward his wife and says:) I can understand now what you have been saying that I have always tried to make you see things my way.

Pastor: But you continue to clam up when she attacks you, like you did a while ago.

Another significant finding of the study mentioned above was that therapists who offered high levels of the facilitative conditions usually confronted the person *with his resources rather than his limitations.* Those therapists who functioned at low levels tended to do just the opposite —i.e., to confront the person with his limitations. This may be due in part, the author conjectured, to the conflicting feelings of the therapist.

What are the implications of this study for the pastoral counselor? Confrontation may increase the person's self-exploration, *if* the facilitative conditions are present.

If they are not, such confrontation may make the person feel he is "being ignored, interrupted, criticized," and/or blocked in his communication.

In addition to the examples given, the pastor's confrontation may be in teaching, imparting information or correcting misinformation, or any other mode of offering the other a "responsible self" against which the other may test his selfhood. Thus, confrontation prompts the person to be honest with himself and with the pastor and enables him to check his views against the pastor, who becomes a significant counterforce.

An example of the pastor's confrontation through teaching is as follows:

Man, age forty-five: My wife is seeing a psychologist, but I want to see somebody in charge of the whole business. I want you to coordinate this thing.

Pastor: You mean you want me to control their counseling sessions? Wouldn't that be bad ethics as well as lack of respect for them as persons? I am wondering whether you heard exactly what your wife said a minute ago—that she feels you constantly try to manipulate her.

Imparting information or correcting misinformation are ways of confronting the person which are basically clarifying in intent:

Man, age thirty-seven: (Angrily) My wife said you said I needed psychiatric help. Is that true?

Pastor: Are you sure you were hearing her correctly? She asked me if I would see you. I assured her I would, if you were agreeable to talking with me. Later she asked me if I thought you needed psychiatric help. I said I didn't know— that would have to be decided between you and me.

Man: Then you did leave the possibility open?

Pastor: How could I make any statements, not having seen you?

Man: OK, I guess you couldn't. (He relaxes and sits back in the chair.)

This is a meeting of hostile confrontation with confrontation. The man was so sensitive and volatile that he came to see the pastor out of resentment. His wife insisted she had said nothing about his seeing a psychiatrist—that he had introduced the idea when he reacted to her suggestion they see someone together.

I was imparting information in the following encounter with several laymen one evening during a group session. Mr. Senn, about thirty-five years of age and a machine operator in one of the city's industrial firms, is speaking:

Mr. Senn: I heard that you fellows at the seminary are beginning a program of mental health training for ministers. Does that mean you are trying to replace the psychiatrists?

Mr. Colston: On the contrary. We are trying to set up structures whereby ministers can have the supervised experience of working *with* psychiatrists and others like social workers, phychologists, and so on. They may be already working with such people, but we are just trying to bring what they are doing into sharper focus, so they can get a better understanding of their own function.

Mr. Mott, in his late twenties, a businessman, speaks up: OK, but aren't you guys really trying to snatch power in the community? Aren't you trying to get in the driver's seat again?

Mr. Colston: "Again?" What do you mean, "again"? (Several members of the group laugh.)

Mr. Mott: Well, the clergy was there once, you know—

back in history—maybe you are trying to get back some of that power you lost! (He laughs.)

Mr. Colston: Oh, you put it straight, don't you! (All laugh.) Well, I must say I was not conscious of that motive, if it's there. But, what's wrong with going for power, if its used responsibly—like doing something constructive for the community? Some kind of power is involved in about anything you do, isn't it?

Mr. Mott: Well, probably so. We just wondered what you are up to.

Mr. Senn: Yeah. We don't want you guys to get too cocky about it.

The laymen were prodding me in good humor to talk about a subject with which they knew I was absorbed. Thus they provided me with an opportunity to impart information in which they were indeed interested, but about which also they could raise questions and subject me to kidding at the same time.

The pastor's confrontation gives the person a point of view against which he can test his own. If the pastor has truly established a facilitating climate, the person may feel free to accept or reject the pastor's point of view as well as accept or reject his own. He is thus helped to become discerning and discriminating in incorporating judgment he receives from others.

The Pastor as Advocate

Facilitation and confrontation presuppose basic concern of person for person. I submit that such actions reflect the vitality of relationships which sustain them. Thus, the pastor mediates what he receives. He is called to stand by the side of the other out of the depths of experiencing being stood alongside by the "saints" who have nurtured him. I have used the term *advocate* to connote what is meant by this reality.

The word is used in the Gospel of John as a translation of the Greek term *Paraclete*, also a designation of the Holy Spirit: "If you love me you will obey my commands; and I will ask the Father, and he will give you another to be your Advocate, who will be with you for ever—the Spirit of truth." (John 14:15-16 NEB.)

The advocate is one who will not forsake the other when the going gets rough. He stands by the person, helping him to remove noxious conditions of self-worth, thus enabling him to experience the release of creative energies. He thus assists the person in abandoning his defenses, alibis, face-saving devices, and in "accepting acceptance."

In his book *Atonement and Psychotherapy*, Don S. Browning explicates four ways in which judgment operates in the therapeutic situation. The first is that of the therapeutic relationship itself. As a situation in which no conditions prevail, it is a judgment upon the person's own conditions for his self-justification and worth. The second is the contradiction between the person's conditions of worth and his experiencing organism. The third has to do with the limitations of the therapist—his limitations as to time and to what invasions of his person and property he can allow from the counselee. These limitations may constitute judgment because they may conflict with the counselee's conditions of worth.

The fourth way in which judgment operates is that with which we are primarily concerned in connection with what we have been saying here. It refers to the immediate relationship between God and man. Browning calls it the "judgment of the structures of integration." "These integrative structures emerge as acts of God performed to actualize an optimum level of integration in the midst of the fallenness of the human situation. They are *contingent* acts that are secondary to the basic essence of God." [10]

These secondary acts of God which are to actualize integration occasion *justice* in the world. They are not contradictory to but are integral to the primary function of God, which is to eventuate a relationship with no conditions, as Browning points out.

Therefore, the pastor mediates the love of God, who accepts the other unconditionally. Justice is not by-passed. On the contrary, in the integrative and responsible acts of man "justice is occasioned in the world."

[10] *Atonement and Psychotherapy* (Philadelphia: Westminster Press, 1966), pp. 200-201.

13   Judgment
in
Pastoral Authority

Pastoral authority arises from the facilitating and confronting interactions among persons who form the *koinonia*—the dedicated community—the church.

As Daniel Day Williams has pointed out, "The minister's representation of the claim and the grace of God is not something which belongs to him simply as an individual, but to him as he stands within the community of believers, the Church, which God has brought into being through his gracious action." [1]

The minister's authority in pastoral counseling is, in large part, derived from the authority of the church. Although I do not wish to give this issue an offhand treatment, my concern with the central theme limits the possibility of adequate discussion of it. I can only deal with it summarily, noting its vital importance to any consideration of pastoral authority. Suffice it to say, I am in basic agreement with Robert S. Paul, who says:

The foundation for the authority we claim, and that which defines its character, is *Christ made contemporary*. The answers are not found in any infallible form of the Church, any infallible hierarchy; nor are they to be found in any infallible book of answers, whether we are tempted to turn

[1] *The Minister and the Care of Souls*, p. 37.

159

to the literal text of the Bible or to the canons of the *Codex Juris Canonici*. We are sent back at every point to the historic figure of our Lord himself, so that through the *magnalia Christi* of the scriptures and church history he may become our Great Contemporary.[2]

What does this mean specifically in regard to the role and function of the minister? Again Dr. Paul frames an answer: "Therefore the authority of a Minister must be essentially *ministerial*, i.e., it must take its character from the Spirit that was in Jesus, to which the Holy Spirit within the Church testifies, and which he seeks to exemplify in us."[3]

Then Paul, quoting from Canon Pythian-Adams adds: "What matters supremely in the Gospel is that *our mutual personal relationships should be those of love*, at whatever cost to ourselves in humiliation, mortification, and long-suffering." He concludes by saying:

Undoubtedly professional competence, historical continuity, and doctrinal orthodoxy are important, and in some measure necessary to a Minister in fulfillment of his vocation, but his authority as a Minister can come only from the source of all authority, and must bear the indelible stamp of Christ's character. A Minister's authority must be judged by its fruits; and the fruits are the fruits of the Spirit.[4]

Commenting on the authority of Jesus, George A. Buttrick wrote the following words in *The Interpreter's Bible*. Buttrick's analysis helpfully sets forth important elements of pastoral authority, upon which I have elaborated:

[2] *Ministry* (Grand Rapids: William B. Eerdmans Publishing Co., 1965), p. 176.
[3] *Ibid.*, p. 190.
[4] *Ibid.*

1. *"He had the authority of silence.* Jesus prayed and pondered. He did not cut himself off from the best wisdom of the past, but he meditated on it in silence until it became his own, in very spirit, not merely in its letter. . . . He . . . spoke from sound intuition." [5]

Thus an essential part of preparation for counseling is silence and prayer, reflection and meditation, wherein the pastor gets perspective upon the moment of encounter and confrontation which is before him. He draws upon the wisdom of the ages, not purely to exhort or instruct, but to make himself ready to accompany the person into the depths of his soul.

2. *"He had the authority of love.* Jesus spoke from a deep fund of compasion. He healed the sick, he played with children, he had a 'great heart.' " [6]

Both judgment and grace proceed from love. Judgment and grace are in polar tension; they are but two sides of the same coin. Functioning within the total context of love, judgment promotes responsibility in all relationships; and grace, through forgiveness and reconciliation, makes such relationships possible. Judgment without love is uncompromising, harsh, demanding, and legalistic; love without judgment is indulgent, pampering, and sentimentalistic.

What applies to love, applies to judgment. Judgment, in love, is slow to lose patience—it looks for a way of being constructive. It is neither anxious to impress nor does it cherish inflated ideas of its own importance; it does not pursue selfish advantage, does not keep account of evil or gloat over the wickedness of other people, but

---

[5] "'The Gospel According to St. Matthew," *The Interpreter's Bible* (Nashville: Abingdon Press, 1951), VII, 335.

[6] *Ibid.,* p. 336.

is glad when truth prevails. It is openhearted, incisive, provocative, and disciplined.

3. *"He had the authority of life.* The face of Jesus was an interpretation of his words; his deeds were of one piece with his commands. His hearers knew there were reserves of soul in him which his teaching had not tapped." [7]

Pastoral counseling is less a matter of technique than it is a matter of life. Who one *is* becomes more important than what he *does.* A disciplined approach to the other, including an honest self-confrontation in light of which he reflectively criticizes his own patterns of relating and deliberately exposes himself to the criticisms of a peer group dedicated to the same process, is the first order of business for the pastoral counselor. This is not to imply that the pastor must engage in slogging self-analysis, only that he be as open to authentic judgment as he expects his parishioners to be.

4. *"He had authority from God.* The springs of truth in him came from a far deeper source than any human probing could find. As people listened, they caught the accent of another world above and beyond and around our world. The eternity in them quickened. Deep called to deep." [8]

The real witness to the pastor's authority is what comes through to the other person, revealing the true quality of the pastor's spirit—the nature of his relationship with God. The ring of authenticity is in the very "sound" of the pastor's life. Those who saw and heard Jesus were convinced he "knew God." However, the "knowing" of God is not just a rational matter. It is being in touch with God's spirit.

One instance showing the dynamics of pastoral authority is as follows:

[7] *Ibid.*
[8] *Ibid.*

The case concerns a pastor who had been counseling a fifteen-year-old girl. One evening she appeared at his home, almost hysterical and threatening suicide. She said she had a "fight" with her parents and never wanted to go back home. She had arrived at the pastor's home a little past eleven o'clock. By the time he could get her quieted down, it was after midnight. The pastor had insisted that he call her parents and tell them she was at his home. She begged him not to call, saying she had hidden some sleeping pills and while he was calling she would take them. He informed her that he would ask his wife to keep an eye on her, but that he must call them. When she saw that he intended to make the call over her protests, she consented. However, although he tried several times, he received no answer. He decided to drive her home. Since he had several small children, his wife could not accompany them. This factor was to contribute to the complexity of the situation.

When the pastor and the girl arrived at her home, they were met by the police, whom the parents had enlisted in a search for her. The pastor explained what had happened in his home; the police, who, seeing that the girl was safely returned, departed to another call. The parents coolly thanked the pastor and took their sullen daughter inside. The pastor was mildly surprised at their attitude toward him. He had known that they were associated with a group which opposed him on many issues, but he did not understand their hostility on this occasion.

The following week, at the meeting of the church board, the parents of the girl, both members of the board, were unfriendly to him. The mother was outspoken in her hostility. The pastor asked the pastoral relations committee of the church to meet within a few days. He also asked that they invite the parents, whom I will call Mr. and Mrs. Honn. An excerpt from that meeting follows:

Chairman: Perhaps you wish to begin, Pastor.

Pastor: It seemed expedient to call this meeting. Apparently I have offended the Honns in some way. I tried to call them and talk to them after I sensed something was in the wind at the board meeting the other night. I did not wish to bring it out there. It seemed more appropriate to talk things out here. Of course, such matters are this committee's responsibility. As far as I can tell, the Honns are upset about Polly (their daughter).

Mrs. Honn: We weren't going to bring it up, but since you seem to want to bring everything out into the open, we'll speak up. (She turns to other members of the group.) Our daughter has been seeing the pastor for several weeks. He's all she talks about. We don't know what's going on, but she scared the living daylights out of us the other night, and here he came driving up with her.

Pastor: What are you getting at, Mrs. Honn?

Mrs. Honn: That we don't know what's going on between you and our daughter.

Pastor: (Quickly and firmly, but quietly) I can tell you. I have been counseling with her.

Mr. Honn: Whatever you are doing, she's getting harder to deal with every day. (To one of the other members) I never did trust him. He hardly ever preaches the Bible.

Mr. Acton: (one of the committee members) That isn't the issue right now, is it, Jake?

Mrs. Honn: She stayed at his house practically all night the other night, and we were worried half to death.

Pastor: Actually, I knew you would be. I tried to call several times after we got her rather settled down. I finally convinced her to come home and drove her. I was not really surprised to learn you had the police looking for her. I'm sure I would have done the same.

This interchange went on for several minutes with the Honns making repeated innuendos regarding the pastor's alleged indiscretions with their daughter. Finally the chairman spoke to the pastor.

Chairman: Perhaps it would be a good idea to get the co-operation of the parents of these teen-age kids you work with from the very beginning, if you can.

Pastor: Yes, it seems that way. I suppose it does appear to the Honns that I was taking her side. Actually, I was trying to help her in her relationships with her parents. I can see now I should have tried to consult with them before I did.

Mr. Murry: (another committee member) It seems to me, though, the pastor is due an apology for the insinuations that he was not behaving properly toward Polly. I don't see any evidence of that, and I think that needs to be cleared up all around town.

Mr. Honn: Are you saying we are talking about him?

Mr. Murry: No, but I am saying somebody is, because I've heard it, and I don't see how he couldn't have. I think if we have got anything to say, we ought to say it here.

Mr. Honn: (to the pastor) Well, I guess we were probably wrong about you, but I wish you would let us handle Polly after this.

Pastor: Naturally, I think you should be the ones to guide her. But let me ask you, do you really feel that I am turning her against you?

Mr. Honn: I don't know, but after she is around you, she is especially hard to manage.

Pastor: How do you mean that?

For several minutes both Mr. and Mrs. Honn entered into an interchange with the pastor. Sensing that some reconciliation had begun to take place, the chairman closed the meeting.

The pastor has received support and gentle chiding from members of the pastoral relations committee. He accepted the chairman's suggestion that he recognize parental responsibility by resolving to do what he could to make early contact with parents of troubled children and seek to elicit their cooperation in a "family-centered" approach.

Polly, the daughter, exhibited several clues to behavior which may be regarded as more complex than adolescent rebellion and warranted his consulting with a psychiatrist as to possible indications that referral might be in order.

The pastor's authority was being strengthened where necessary and supported where appropriate by members of the pastoral relations committee. The Honns also were given an opportunity to face up to their learning possibilities. Improved relationships with the pastor and probably with members of the committee were the result.

As I have cited from Daniel Day Williams' view of pastoral authority, judgment is in the pastor's representation of the claim of God which is put alongside the gift of God. These phrases are another way of showing the interrelatedness of the judgment and grace of God. The pastor who learns to maintain a healthy tension between these two concepts in his basic attitudes and understanding embodies a pastoral authority which witnesses to its very source!

The Pastor's Acceptance as Judgment

Even acceptance can be a form of judgment and perceived as threatening. Seward Hiltner has pointed out that the psychiatrist's acceptance of the patient or the clinical psychologist's acceptance of the client is received ambiguously, that when the patient feels the psychiatrist accepts him, he also feels most threatened.[9]

Previously the client had felt that if the counselor really knew what he was like, he would not accept him. He had put most of his energies into defending what he regarded as unacceptable in himself. Now that this part is accepted, he is thrown into a quandary. He faces new responsibility, consequently his anxiety is raised and he feels threatened. He is torn between the feeling of release and a sense of loss of the old defenses and the obligation of his new responsibility. He experiences the relief of having the bonds of slavery to his old defensive patterns severed, but he is uncertain what to do with his newfound freedom, especially in relation to the one who has set him free.

The pastoral theologian, dealing with such data will carry his questions further. He may well say in this type of situation it would appear that just when love that has long been offered is finally recognized and received as love, at precisely that moment does judgment seem to be felt most terribly. The depth of one's unacceptability is recognized only as this has been accepted by something not of one's own creation.[10]

The pastor, therefore, should not be greatly surprised if his reaching out in love to the person is received by that person as judgment and threat. The person who has long regarded himself as unworthy now experiences the pastor's positive judgment of his worth, which is contradictory to his prevailing view of himself. He either finds the acceptance hard to believe—consequently, does not trust it—or he rejects it outright.

[9] *Preface to Pastoral Theology* (Nashville: Abingdon Press, 1958), pp. 27-29.
[10] *Ibid.,* p. 29.

Strange as it may seem, the person may actually panic, because what were once reliable defenses are of no further use to him. If he accepts the acceptance, something is required of him, not the least of which is a total revision of his self-concept. He is left without excuse, which in itself is a manifestation of judgment. He can no longer alibi, "I am unlovable because I am unloved; therefore don't expect anything from me."

For example, Miss Booley, a twenty-seven-year-old single woman, had been referred to me by a local pastor. She was extremely shy, although she worked regularly in the business office of a small industry in the town. Although she was not beautiful by any criteria which are usually applied, she was not unattractive. However, she had few men friends and seemed unable to attract men.

She had painfully and laboriously managed to bring out a number of self-effacing assertions about herself, and to express feelings of hopelessness about being effective in her interpersonal relationships. I found myself literally pulling feelings out of her, despite the fact that she was sufficiently motivated to keep each appointment promptly and regularly.

At the beginning of the fourth interview she reported the following dream to me:

Miss Booley: It seemed to be along a seashore. I was walking in the sand. There was a gentle breeze. I was along the edge of the water, letting the waves, which were almost at the end of their rush, flow gently over my bare feet. I remember I was feeling serene and calm. Suddenly, I became vaguely aware of a shadow on one side of me. Startled, I looked up and saw a figure coming toward me. I became frightened and started running along the beach.

I was aware somehow that the figure was following me, although, I recall, I was too scared to look back. As I ran, I saw what looked like a beach house, just ahead of me and not far to the right. It seemed to be a queer house, sort of like a box. Many questions seemed to be racing through my mind. Would I be trapped if I went in there? But wouldn't I be surely caught if I didn't? Perhaps I could get in and close the door quickly. So I made the dash for the beach house and closed the door with a sign of relief. But as I turned around, I saw that there was no back or sides to the house, only a front with a door in it, like a movie scene, you know? There was this figure, just standing, looking at me. At that moment I woke up. My heart was beating wildly, and I was perspiring something terrible. I worried about the dream all day.

Mr. Colston: Does it have a meaning to you?

Miss Booley: (She blushes deeply and speaks with great effort, not facing me, and toying nervously with the handle of her purse.) Well, I finally decided that the figure on the beach must represent you. I've thought if coming here is going to cause me that much pain, I'd better reconsider. Yet coming seems to help, too, so you see, I came back. (She gestures and smiles.)

Here I am concerned only to show how acceptance can be perceived as judgment. Miss Booley apparently was being threatened by my persistent "pulling out" of her feelings and was fearful of being trapped. Although she seemed to wish to avoid facing me, there was a part of her which would not let her escape such confrontation.

The pastor's acceptance may be rejected, but it provides the emotional bridge across which the person can cross to meet the pastor. If the pastor understands that the extension of his love may be threatening to the person and patiently reveals that understanding, the bridge will become strengthened in trust, and will carry the weight of continued encounter. However, to push the metaphor further in line with our theme of judgment, eventually considerable "jousting" may take place on the bridge, but, as in the days when it was a popular sport, the aim is not necessarily to destroy the combatant, but to test his strength. Such testing by the counselee will quite likely occur as he seeks to determine the authority of the pastor and his power to stay with him in the encounter.

The Pastor's Evaluation as Judgment

As the pastor confronts the person, he invariably does some evaluating of the person. Likewise, unquestionably the person evaluates the pastor. However, since we are discussing the pastor's function as counselor, we will limit ourselves for the moment to that aspect of the interaction. Pertinent questions are: What kinds of evaluations serve the pastoral counseling process and which render a distinct disservice? What is the relationship of evaluation to diagnosis and to what degree is the pastor involved in the latter?

In a paper entitled "The Goals of Counseling," John M. Butler wrote a section on the evaluative attitudes of the counselor. Distinguishing between *prizing* and *appraising*, he asserts that nonevaluative behavior in the counselor is evaluative behavior of a special kind.

Prizing designates activities such as honoring, holding precious or dear, regarding highly, treasuring. . . . Appraising on the other hand involves putting a value on or assigning a value to. . . . Discriminations are involved in appraising; they are not involved in prizing. . . . In a word, the counselor is un-

170

critical and undiscriminating *in his behavior* with respect to the person of the client.[11]

Certainly "prizing" the person is of top priority in attitudes which serve the counseling function. Clarification is needed here. Granted, the sensitive counselor does not discriminate against the person as person. However, he may fulfill the person's desire for an external authority against which and with which his own authority may be tested and strengthened. He may also discern the person's need for assuming responsibility and strive to provide the push which may prompt the person to act on his own judgment.

Butler goes on to say there are a number of valuings in the counseling hour: "The counselor himself receives gratification and satisfaction from the human dignity, uniqueness, and trend toward growth or self-improvement of the client." [12] This acknowledges that the counselor does gain satisfaction from his counseling. We may add, particularly if he has acted as an effective catalyst in the trend toward growth or is triggering action toward self-improvement in the person, especially if that means his becoming more responsible as a person.

Assessing is in the service of counseling if the assessment is for the purpose of determining where the person is in the process of the assimilation of judgment. Then the pastor can help the person who may be bogging down in a particular stage to get off dead center.

Diagnosing is also in the service of counseling, if employed in its literal sense. "To diagnose is to differentiate,

---

[11] An unpublished paper in the Counseling Center Discussion Papers of the University of Chicago, 1956, II, 5.
[12] *Ibid.*, p. 8.

to distinguish, to designate. It is to recognize, to have knowledge of, to come to an understanding of." [13] For the pastor to diagnose does not necessarily mean he will become involved in painstaking measures for narrowing down data presented him into diagnostic categories; rather that he may recognize symptoms of deep intrapsychic conflicts which require greater time and effort in differentiation than his pastoral duties will allow. If, for example, he sees a person in a continued depressive state, his diagnostic judgment is to help the person get the psychiatric treatment he needs.

The pastor may also work as a member of a "treatment team" in community mental health, helping the person "to come out" in ways appropriate to his own development. In this regard, he may be auxiliary to the diagnostic process. He may make a singular contribution to what Karl Menninger regards as the fundamental purpose of diagnosis.

Diagnosis has gradually become a matter less of seeking to identify a classical picture and give it a name than of understanding the way in which an individual has been taken with a disability, partly self-imposed and partly externally brought about.[14]

Menninger thus notes the real complexity of diagnosis. He points to the polar tension between individual freedom and determinism. Thus he suggests the true "diagnostic" dimensions of pastoral counseling. The pastor, along with other members of the helping professions, is called upon not only to distinguish the way an individual has a self-imposed disability, but also the ways in which family and

---

[13] Karl Menninger, *The Vital Balance,* p. 36.
[14] *Ibid.,* p. 35.

community contribute to that disability. In other words, true diagnosis must take place in the total context of the disability. Thus social ills come under the diagnostic purview as well as the personal ills with which they are interrelated. Furthermore, the term *krino* in the *Theological Dictionary of the New Testament* is interpreted as follows:

What is unconditionally demanded is that such evaluations should be subject to the certainty that God's judgment falls also on those who judge, so that superiority, hardness, and blindness to one's own faults are excluded, and a readiness to forgive and to intercede is safeguarded.[15]

The spirit in which judgment as evaluation is undertaken is crucial. If either personal or social judgment is retaliatory and condemnatory, it is a judgment which is severally judged. However, if it is in the spirit of forgiveness and reconciliation and accompanied by the desire to intercede, judgment is productive and necessary.

The Mutuality of Judgment

A warranted change on the part of any counselor consciously or unconsciously impressed with his own helping role is from a condescending to a "con-discerning" attitude toward the counselee, when discernment is regarded as synonymous with discrimination in the sense of differentiated judgment. This is another way of saying that the person is treated as "thou" rather than an "it." The pastor discerns along with the parishioner, not for him or against him. It is a joint enterprise in which both are deeply involved, not to the degree that the identity of either is lost,

[15] Vol. III, p. 939.

but, on the contrary, the identities of both are affirmed and enhanced. Thus, the pastor communicates his fundamental respect for the person's right of personal judgment while asserting his own and maintaining his confidence in the work of the Spirit throughout. A "con-discerning" attitude is manifest in the spirit of love and positive regard for the parishioner.

In a discussion of the role of the physician in the illness-recovery process, Karl Menninger speaks of "the intangibles" in the doctor-patient relationship. Drawing on the classic statement of the apostle Paul on love, he asserts that love is one of the great intangibles in the effective functioning of the psychiatrist. He states that transference and countertransference can have destructive effects as well as constructive ones. He then says:

The doctor and the whole therapeutic milieu should aim at replacing the emotional transference judgment with an objective judgment—not through arguments, not through reasoning, not through contradiction, but through example; not through indiscriminate permissiveness or coercion but through the use of measures which increase the patient's self-confidence.[16]

This applies equally well to the pastoral counselor. His love breaks through the distorted images or unrealistic expectations which the counselee has of him or of his functions. Through the manifestation of his own being and genuine positive regard for the person, he demonstrates the discriminative character of his judgment and reinforces that of the other. Measures which increase the confidence of the parishioner are generated in a climate of love and

[16] *The Vital Balance*, p. 364.

acceptance so that even negative judgments are less to condemn than to upbuild. Thus, the person confronting the sincere trust communicated by the pastor can find his trust in himself restored.

I wish to emphasize, however, that the need for developing skills in pastoral counseling and in the pastor's ability to judge when referral is in order warrants the pastor's insistence that he have at least some basic experience in a clinical setting. Intensive training in clinical pastoral education and pastoral counseling under the supervision of a chaplain or counselor who has been certified by one of the national accrediting and certifying associations concerned with setting high standards for pastoral care and counseling[17] is a significant preparation for a discerning counseling ministry and for orienting the minister to referral agencies. Thus, he not only develops his own skills; he learns his strengths and limitations; he becomes more acutely aware of the functions of the members of other helping professions and, hopefully, how better to cooperate with them.

The Minister and the Church

As I emphasized early in this chapter and as Williams has asserted in his discussion of the minister's authority, no view of the ministry can be considered adequate if it does not presuppose the representative character of the ministerial office.

There are very different views of how the representative character of the office is established in the Church, and there

[17] Such as the Association for Clinical Pastoral Education, and the American Association of Pastoral Counselors.

are different views of the way in which the authority it involves is conferred and can be exercised. But we see in every actual ministry an office and a vocation which involve the special responsibility of the Christian minister for presenting to the church and representing in the church the ministry of Christ which brought the Church into being.[18]

It is important to note the dialogical character of the interpretation of the ministry of Christ which Williams is suggesting. The minister not only *represents* but also *presents* that ministry. He is expected at once to embody and to interpret the healing ministry of Christ to his congregation. This means he "has to learn to divest himself and his language at times of just these recognizable symbols (of his public vocation) in order to help people recover their real meaning." [19]

One of the criticisms leveled at the minister today by thousands of people trapped in ghettos of large cities is that he hides behind his clerical and professional symbols to escape the real issues. To the degree that this accusation is true—and who can say how much of a real indictment it is?—the minister is challenged to come out and face the discipline of human life and experience.

What should be the pastor's fundamental goal in his continuing education for this task? It may be put simply in the words of the apostle Paul: "Let us therefore cease judging one another, but rather make this simple judgment: that no obstacle or stumbling block be placed in a brother's way" (Rom. 14:13 NEB.). Paul's exhortation to the Romans would seem to contradict what we have been saying; actually it supports our view. We are to

[18] *The Minister and the Care of Souls*, p. 34.
[19] *Ibid.*, p. 47.

cease irresponsible, ill considered, and offhand judgments, or those which are designed to reinforce our own prejudices and position, for the sake of a discerning judgment. "Simple" is not meant to be synonomous with "easy, not requiring effort," but with "fundamental," "uncomplex," "at the heart." Thus the "simple" judgment requires great discipline to remove the "blocks" and "trips" in the pastor's approach to the person. He thus facilitates the person's capacity to assimilate the judgment he faces.

14 Judgment in the Household of God

The pastor not only derives authority from the community he serves, he also gives authority and leadership to it. He functions as facilitator, enabler, confronter, and provocator of the laity. "Equipping the saints" is the biblical term given to the whole task, which is to call out and prepare each one for his essential vocation of glorifying God through his care and service.

He gives leadership to the reinforcement of integrating structures within the community as well as within each person. The community (*koinonia*) thus formed has expanded its consciousness to encompass what the apostle Paul has called "the household of God." The Spirit works in and through that community, giving vitality and dimension to it. One of the distinguishing characteristics of that community is its view of its life from the perspective of ultimate meanings and values. The person finds his identity and purpose within that community. He transcends the community and lives in tension with it, yet one can never really understand a man without knowing his relations to it. What is the nature of the "household of God?"

A Mediating Community

Each man lives in some degree of tension with the particular community of which he is apart, because he sees it both as fulfillment and frustration. He can't live with it, and he can't live without it. He may exchange his loyalty to one community for another, which he may regard as more fulfilling, but he continually stands in relationship to some community, whose values he accepts and by whom, to some degree, he measures himself. If he does not, he suffers the pain of isolation and faces the threat of disintegration. Even if he rejects the values of his community, he is living in relation to them.

A theological student in a group of fellow students was continually attacking members of the group whom he regarded as conservative. One of the other students observed that this practice had become a "thing" with the student to the degree that he wondered why. Another perceived that the student was overreacting to his own "conservative" background. "I guess you aren't as emancipated as you keep saying," the latter said.

Later in the session the student admitted to the group, "My wife keeps telling me when I get back home—you know back in my home community—I am a totally different person. I haven't seen it, but I am beginning to see what she—and you—are talking about. I am two different people. I suppose I'll have to figure out how to get me together. (He laughs.) I am just now seeing that my background is more a part of me than I was willing to admit."

The student was beginning to reconcile the striking differences between his intellectual and emotional reactions. Thus, during the entire session, he was at least aware of and dealing with data associated with the first three stages of judgment. He was at the point where testing out what he had learned would be the logical next step.

Now, if I am asked, How are judgment and grace mediated? I answer, Through the community of faith which reverences the mystery of interpersonal communion (*koinonia*) and is dedicated to the work of reconciliation. Clearly, biblical references to the nature of the church consistently employ the terms *koinonia* and *diakonia* to designate functions appropriate to the church's ministry. In view of the auspicious role of the community of faith in the mediation of judgment and grace, the admonition to the church in I Peter 4:17 is as timely and pertinent as it was when it was originally addressed to the church: "For the time has come for judgment to begin with the household of God; and if it begins with us, what will be the end of those who do not obey the gospel of God?"

The household of God is the community which has been brought low by the law of God and raised by his grace. Thus, it is the course for the new life which is effected through the assimilation of judgment and the resulting transformation it brings. It lays claim to the legitimacy of its family ties through the authenticity of its own life. The household of God is that as long as it is in a living relationship with God, by whom its functions are judged.

The *Theological Dictionary of the New Testament* makes the following statement regarding judgment: "Precisely the unreserved seriousness with which the community takes the concept of judgment in the Gospel is that which enables it to overcome a mere legalism in its religious and moral life."[1] Religious discipline and persistent dedication are required to effect a sharply differentiated and relevant judgment. Mere legalism is an attempt to short-circuit the process. It requires less strain and intellectual effort, less troublesome concern with ambiguity, but it produces "cribbed," rigid, and tyrannical individuals as a consequence.

[1] Vol. III, p. 940.

180

Mutually Correcting and Supporting

The truly redemptive community is one in which mutual judgment and reinforcement add to the stature and potentiality of each member. "Brethren, if a man is overtaken in a trespass, you who are spiritual should restore him in a spirit of gentleness . . . Bear one another's burdens," says Paul. "Each man will have to bear his own load." (Gal. 6: 1, 2, 6.) The critical balance between dependency and independency is maintained through judgment in the context of love. Just as in the household of a family the father reproves his son, not to alienate him, but to help him become a responsible member of the family by "bearing his own burdens" and the burdens of others, the Christian community or the household of God performs a similar function.

The self-asserting and self-denying tendencies in man find their harmony in those who by personal devotion to Christ are drawn together and united to one another. Judgment in the context of the redemptive community upbuilds the members who in faith and love meet each other in common trust rather than in mistrust and suspicion; judgment in this context means a discerning appreciation of justice made manifest in the wrath and love of God.

Earlier we discussed the term *krisis,* showing its biblical uses in conveying the idea of judgment. Now we will see it in its combined form—*hypokrisis*—having the general meaning in the New Testament of pretending to be what one is not. Defining the term in relation to guilt, David Belgum has stated that "hypocrisy thwarts the church's ministry of healing." [2] He draws out a hypothetical church

[2] David Belgum, *Guilt: Where Psychology and Religion Meet.* (Englewood Cliffs, N.J.: Prentice-Hall, 1963), p. 12.

with a thousand members, 170 of whom are in serious emotional trouble and who must turn elsewhere for help because in many cases the church is simply not a redemptive fellowship, hypocritical attitudes prevail.

What would be the nature of a hypothetical church in which the thousand members believed that they had, individually, as the Scripture says, "sinned and fall[en] short of the glory of God"? They would each be ready to join in the battle against sin, to aid their fallen brother in the resolution of his guilt, and to support him in victorious living; and there would be a very good chance for victory." [3]

Another point at which the household of God incurs judgment is in regard to its function of *reconciliation*. Reconciliation is effected through genuine responses to human need in healing and serving. The church in many instances has not only relinquished its reconciliatory mission to other agencies and groups, but also, unfortunately, has contributed to the alienation of people and groups within our culture either by actually fostering negative attitudes toward them or by simply ignoring them.

The judgment which the church, at least in some of its manifestations, is acknowledging is that it has tried to put its new understanding into "old wineskins." New forms of *koinonia* are now being recognized and encouraged. Industrial missions and action training centers are emerging. They are seeking to establish and maintain communication among the widely dispersed and the heavily concentrated populations in our sprawling industrialized metropolitan areas and to fulfill the reconciling mission of the Christian community.

[3] *Ibid.,* p. 15.

A Redeeming Body

A metaphor which the apostle Paul repeatedly employed to describe the church was "the body of Christ." The organic nature of the *koinonia* was explicitly declared in the twelfth chapter of I Corinthians, for example:

> But God has so adjusted the body, giving the greater honor to the inferior part, that there may be no discord in the body, but that the members may have the same care for one another. If one member suffers, all suffer together; if one member is honored, all rejoice together. Now you are the body of Christ and individually members of it. (I Cor. 12:24-27.)

In regard to Christ's relationship to the organism: "He is the head of the body, the church; he is the beginning, the firstborn from the dead, that in everything he might be preëminent" (Col. 1:18).

The church is thus depicted as Christ's continuing incarnation in the world. The fundamental task and primary responsibility is to generate and nourish his spirit everywhere, "until the whole of life becomes a like organism, illumined, inspired, controlled, and dominated by the Lord of all good life." [4] In effect, the whole of humanity is urged to become a church.

The judgment inherent in the functioning organism is abundantly clear: if one suffers, all suffer; if one is honored, all are honored. To help another grow is to help one's self grow; likewise, to gain strength and wisdom in one's self is to add such qualities to the whole organism. To be responsible is to engender responsibility and to give life and vitality to the larger organism.

---

[4] John Short, "The First Epistle to the Corinthians," *The Interpreter's Bible* (Nashville: Abingdon Press, 1953), X, 158.

A group of ministers had been in therapy sessions for several weeks. In the session cited below, two of the men, whom I will call John Metts and Ray Vonn, finally came into a head-on encounter. Just prior to the interchange which follows, Ray Vonn had replied to Art Romm. John Metts was visibly uncomfortable with what was taking place. He breaks in:

Metts: Well, that's all well and good—what you are saying to Art—but as Calvin has put it . . .

Vonn: (He leans forward toward John Metts.) John, when are you going to stop hiding behind Calvin? (Facetiously) "Will the real John please stand up?" (He sits back in his chair and gestures imploring toward Metts.) I mean—man —when are we going to meet you? We have been getting together now—what—about four times? But I don't know you yet.

Metts: (His face reddens and he sits stunned. Finally he speaks in a hurt tone.) Does my Calvinism bug you?

Vonn: You are not hearing me, John. You are implying I'm prejudiced against Calvinism. I'm just saying I think you are hiding behind it. Maybe if you were a really good Calvinist you wouldn't need to. (He shrugs.)

Metts: (He sits quietly for a moment eyeing Ray Vonn intently. Finally he speaks softly but firmly.) I must say, Ray, of all the men here, you are the one I have had the greatest doubts about.

Vonn: You don't approve of me?

Metts: Well, let's just say I rarely find myself agreeing with you.

Vonn: Is that what you want—for me to agree with you?

Metts: Not necessarily. I'm not concerned about that. It's whether or not we are Christ's that's important.

Vonn: Oh, come on now. Let's not get in that hang-up. Of

course, that's important, but what I am concerned about has fundamentally to do with you and me. You have some strong feelings about me. My theology seems to be mixed up in it, but what are we really talking about?

The dialogue continued in this manner for several minutes with other members of the group entering in occasionally. After the session, the two men went to their dormitory rooms, where they talked until late that night. The following day, they returned to the group.

John Metts speaks first:

Metts: Last night was quite an experience for me. I didn't think I could even talk to a "liberal," let alone have a good feeling for him, like I do now for Ray. I am changing my image of him—in fact I am feeling different toward all of you fellows.

Vonn: This goes for me, too. Talking to John has helped me to discover some of my blind spots. I have been inclined to ridicule what I regard as naïveté. John has helped me to see that I am fighting that in myself.

Equally evident is the importance of the individual members to the body. No one is regarded as inferior or of lesser rank, although his functions may not be as highly developed as those of another. As in the case of the human body, each part has its significant and particular function. Although loss of some of the parts may not be fatal to the human body, any loss may handicap the body and require compensation. Just because the hand is not the eye, this does not mean the hand is of less consequence to the organism than the eye.

The head of the body is Christ, who gives the organism perspective on its existence and direction as to its meaning and purpose. The head of the body gives it self-conscious awareness of its history and destiny and establishes the unity of its existence.

Speaking of judgment in relation to questions of the practice of religion, Paul says to the Colossians:

Let no one disqualify you, insisting on self-abasement and worship of angels . . . and not holding fast to the Head, from whom the whole body, nourished and knit together through its joints and ligaments, grows with a growth that is from God. (Col. 2:18, 19.)

A similar idea is contained in the fourth chapter of Ephesians:

Rather, speaking the truth in love, we are to grow up in every way into him who is the head, into Christ, from whom the whole body, joined and knit together by every joint with which it is supplied, when each part is working properly, makes bodily growth and upbuilds itself in love. (Eph. 4:15-16.)

Contiguity is not a guarantor of communication. Just bringing people together does not automatically produce conversation or assure that they will talk with each other. Communication is the act of openhearted confrontation. "Speaking the truth in love" opens the way to community, which is brought into being through communication. We are matured in the act of sharing fully in the common life.

A brief excerpt from a series of conversations with a group of Negro lay persons illustrates what is meant here. I was invited to meet with the group in their Wednesday evening Prayer and Dialogue sessions over a period of several weeks.

The first session was pleasant but rather uneventful. The second also began in a polite and, obviously patronizing tone. One of the men, about fifty-five years of age, who had spoken very little during the first meeting, suddenly addressed the group:

Mr. Geun: Why don't we stop walking on eggs? As I feel it we're all tightened up here. I don't know about the rest of you, but I've got to say what I think. I have the feeling some of us are saying nice words we don't really believe in.

Mrs. Norr: Well, maybe we do, George.

Mr. Geun: Maybe. Let's see if you do. Anyway I didn't say I am talking for you, I am just speaking for myself, Mrs. Norr. (He laughs.) Well, anyway, I have a lot of bad feelings toward the white man which just didn't get there overnight. (He looks at me.) Now you got a nice smile, and I'd like to believe it—but—you see I got these feelings down deep inside that just don't let me. It's just—I find it hard to trust any white man.

Mr. Colston: I gather you'd like to feel you can trust me, but—

Mr. Geun: Yeah. When you've had to rustle food out of garbage cans and worry every minute about whether somebody's going to get you—well—it kind of gets in your blood. It's been bothering me here, that we haven't been telling you "like it is."

Mr. Colston: I am feeling the strain, too. I have been trying so hard to show you that I am not prejudiced that it makes me wonder if I am not trying to convince myself. (The members of the group laugh.)

The group quickly became more relaxed. Several who had not previously spoken began to interact with us and other members of the group. The closing prayer by one of the members was spontaneous and genuinely expressive of gratitude for the occasion.

The task of establishing community among a group of people whose own egotisms or self-interests multiply the possibilities of clash and conflict is not accomplished simply by an agreement to meet on a common ground. The New Testament speaks of dying to self, which is repentance. The true *koinonia*, or household of God, is composed of repentant and forgiven sinners. Even their cherished preconceptions are transformed.

The central figure of the gospel—the dying and rising Christ—provides the paradigm for the organism and for the members which comprise it. Repentance is analogous with "the dying"; forgiveness with "the rising." Repentance is the act of giving up the self, but this is not an acquiescence; it is the yielding of conditions which block the self from realizing true integrity. The persistent justifying of alienating attitudes in the self are not for the sake of integrity, although the self may be deceived into believing so. Repentance is the first step toward restoring harmony and unity to the organism. Forgiveness is already at work.

15 Judgment and Forgiveness

Judgment is not the final word. I began with the assumption that *judgment is love at the right time*. Now, I will add: *forgiveness is love throughout time*. Love flows from gratitude for forgiveness. The writer who addresses the Christians in the first letter of John puts the matter thusly:

> For God is love; and his love was disclosed to us in this, that he sent his only Son into the world to bring us life. The love I speak of is not our love for God, but the love he showed us in sending his Son as the remedy for the defilement of our sins. If God thus loved us, dear friends, we in turn are bound to love one another. (I John 4:9-11 NEB.)

Here love presupposes gratitude. If a person does not accept or sees no need for forgiveness, he is likely to be unable either to give or to receive love, or to recognize it when its power unfolds before him. For example: when Jesus said to the Pharisee, in the latter's house, "Do you see this woman?" referring to the extremely remorseful woman who had been living an immoral life but who, at that moment, was ministering to him, he was implying judgment. The Pharisee was *not seeing* the woman, nor perceiving the significance of her acts. "Her sins, which are many," Jesus was quoted as saying, "are forgiven, for she loved much; but he who is forgiven little, loves little." (Luke 7:36-50.) The person who stands aloof and preens his righteous feathers runs the risk of little sinfulness, hence does not have much to forgive, but he also suffers the consequences of loving little.

The following is a conversation, which I have reproduced from memory, of an exchange which I had with a thirty-nine-year-old woman. I had known her for several years and, at one time, had several counseling sessions with her. When I perceived that she gave evidence of extreme depression, I had referred her to a psychiatrist. She saw him a few times, then terminated the relationship, saying she didn't need treatment because she was able to function quite well on her own.

Some time later on a summer night, about 2:00 A.M., I received an anxious telephone call from her husband, who said she was insisting that she be hospitalized in a psychiatric ward, but that she would not go unless I went along with them. I agreed to go. I dressed hurriedly and went to their home. I found her in a depressed state, numbly going through rather ineffective motions of packing her clothing.

As we were driving to the hospital, the conversation between us was mainly as follows:

Patricia: People don't really care about each other. They could care less. Oh sure, people do things for each other, but they always want something in return. They've got a price! You can just bet on it. Sometime they're going to come back and say, "Look what I did for you!" Everybody is out to get something. What about you? What's your price? What do you expect to get out of me?

Mr. Colston: Well, the satisfaction of helping you, if I possibly can, Pat.

Patricia: Oh come on, now, what's your real reason? Why did you come over here at this time of the morning to go down here with us?

Mr. Colston: Because you asked your husband to call me, Pat. I figured that it was an S.O.S. and I should come.

Patricia: Well, sure you did, but I still don't know why you came. You haven't answered that.

Mr. Colston: You want to pay me?

Patricia: Yes, I do. (Defiantly she reached for her purse.)

Mr. Colston: You can't pay me. You don't have enough money to buy what I'm giving you.

Patricia: You think you are pretty great, don't you?

Mr. Colston: Not at all. I don't possess it. In fact, it has been given freely to me.

Patricia: What are you talking about?

Mr. Colston: Christian love.

Patricia: Oh, God! Don't give me that religious stuff! You know I don't believe in that.

Mr. Colston: OK, let me put it another way. I have needed help on many occasions. I know how it feels to have someone respond when you need him. Many persons have helped me when I needed it. They neither asked nor seemed to expect anything in return. I am grateful. That's why I'm here. I can never repay the many people who have lost sleep in my behalf, but I can do my part.

Patricia: I don't believe that stuff.

Mr. Colston: I didn't ask you to. You believe I'm here, don't you?

Patricia: Yes.

Mr. Colston: OK, that's all that really matters. Let's go!

Patricia: OK, OK.

Later, I visited her in the hospital. As we were talking, she suddenly said to me, "You know, I've been thinking a great deal about what you said to me."

"Oh?" I replied.

191

"Yes, you know, about your needing help. I hadn't thought of it that way."

"You were rather shocked to hear me say that?"

"Well, maybe. I don't think I was shocked. I just hadn't thought much about you. At first, I didn't like it that you made me aware of you. Then I finally realized I was being selfish. It hadn't occurred to me that you could ever have needed help like I did. Then you said there were a lot of people you had to depend on. I hadn't thought of it that way. I couldn't really believe it. I am not sure I do yet. (She paused.) Anyway, it seems to me that people usually have some hidden something they eventually come out with as a 'price.' I'll have to think about it some more."

Patricia was intellectually rejecting my pastoral office while actually relating to me in terms of it. She had not been viewing me as a person and was somewhat nonplussed when I reminded her of the fact. She consciously drew upon what she regarded as my "strength." She had not thought of me as needing anybody, consequently my confession of weakness came initially as a shock to her. My statement of gratitude for what people had contributed to me made her feel guilty. She later responded by saying, "I finally realized I was being selfish." She had to think about my being there as a small way of paying back a huge debt to many persons who had heeded my cries for help with gratuitous service. To put the key phrase of the story of the woman in the Pharisee's house in another way: He who is forgiven much, loves much.

Communion Is Participation

Affirming the satisfaction and fulfillment he realizes in his commitment to the *koinonia*, Paul says: "Now I rejoice in my sufferings for your sake, and in my flesh I complete what is lacking in Christ's afflictions for the sake of his body, that is, the church" (Col. 1:24).

Commitment to the organism commits one to a degree of suffering, but the increased capacity to love carries with it the increased vulnerability to suffering. Conversely, little love for others means less involvement in their suffering. Of course, it also means an isolated existence in which no love is given and none received. To move toward another in love is to take on his suffering.

Sensitivity to the other and to what he is experiencing can be painful, but ultimately satisfying, because it opens the understanding to the larger context of meaning. As one assimilates the judgment he encounters through being sensitive to the other, he also increases his capacity for the endurance of his own suffering. He even rejoices in it, not in a masochistic sense, but in a sacrificial sense, especially if such suffering is for the sake of the body, which is the *koinonia*, or, as we have been saying here, the household of God.

The biblical imagery of the body of Christ supports our contention that the church is an organism, not an organization. "The congregation is united only through Christ. Its common life derives from common union with Him, not from the common ties between believers. The community is not a pneumatic democracy; it is a pneumatic organism. Its unity is love, not compulsion." [1]

Although I accept the fundamental thrust of this assertion regarding judgment in the church, I hasten to qualify my agreement with it in the following way: the fundamental unity of the community is love, if that is meant in the sense in which we began this whole discussion of judgment, i.e., *if love and justice are seen as going*

[1] *Theological Dictionary of the New Testament,* III, 944.

together. The Christian community is not an organization of persons who have banded themselves together out of purely prudential concerns. It is not a group which has set up a series of ground rules to govern its common life. It is the body of Christ, the incarnation of the Word. Thus, judgment in the Christian community can never be a detached, peripheral kind of concern, but that which reflects its very nature and its very mission—the representation of love and justice in the world.

In a popular best seller, *Games People Play,*[2] Eric Berne raises the ultimately inevitable question, "After games, what?" He concludes that the transcending qualities of "awareness," "spontaneity," and "intimacy" are available to "certain fortunate people." However, these concepts are not unambiguous. For example, spontaneity not held in tension with deliberation runs the risk of irresponsibility. Likewise, intimacy, without its polar relationship to *distantiation,*[3] may give rise to insufferable boredom. Furthermore, one is not soundly aware, spontaneous, and intimate willy-nilly. A central and meaningful focus is required.

Communion is the term which is suggestive of the desirable transcendental goal. Communion is not simply propinquity or proximity—it is participation. This is participation in the lives of others guided by fundamental respect. It is the act of "putting on" one's neighbor—his joys and sorrows, his happiness and sufferings, and so on. All of this assumes a unifying Christology in the world.

The Eucharist, the Lord's Supper or Holy Communion,

[2] Eric Berne, *Games People Play* (New York: Grove Press, 1964), p. 184.

[3] See Erik Erikson's use of the term "distantiation" in a chapter entitled, "Growth and Crises of the 'Healthy Personality,'" in Clyde Kluckhohn and Henry A. Murray, eds., *Personality in Nature, Society, and Culture* (New York: Alfred A. Knopf, 1954), p. 222.

brings the meaning of the organic unity in love into dramatic focus. Our attention is continually and periodically drawn to the reminder of who we are, from whence we have come, and what holds us together. We are reminded also of our central vocation—being called to serve at this moment, at this place, those whom we encounter.

"The cup of blessing which we bless," contends the apostle Paul, "is it not a participation in the blood of Christ? The bread which we break, is it not a participation in the body of Christ?" (I Cor. 10:16.)

The meaning of the Eucharist is thus made clear. In the act of partaking with another, one manifests his comprehension of the bond which exists between them and his commitment to it. It is not only a shared act, but also a shared heritage and destiny to which the act attests.

The Forgiving Community

Acknowledging that he based one of his hypotheses on my previous study of the context of pastoral counseling, James G. Emerson, Jr., asserts: "The contextual nature of the church is that of forgiveness." [4] I accept his statement. However, my assumption throughout this study has been: The contextual nature of the church is appropriately *judgment and forgiveness*. Judgment makes forgiveness necessary; forgiveness make judgment possible. In other words, if a person's conditions for self-worth stand, in some way, between himself and another, he may be reconciled with the other if he repents and receives forgiveness. His judgments of the other, which were distorted, now become more discerning. Forgiveness makes this possible.

[4] Emerson, *The Dynamics of Forgiveness* (Philadelphia: Westminster Press, 1964), p. 31.

195

To illustrate: Mr. Bronn, who did not seem able even to sit facing me in the counseling room, was finally able to move his chair into a position where he could confront me. Evidently as he experienced forgiveness, which he did not see as necessarily coming from me, he regarded me differently. He no longer perceived my judgment in a distorted manner. Not only was Mr. Bronn's *perception* of me changing, his *conception* of God was being transformed at the same time. I represented to him the forgiving community, a community upon which I drew for resources and whose forgiveness I was continually experiencing. As Emerson points out, "There is a positive correlation between forgiveness as experienced and personality as integrated or adjusted." [5] Mr. Brown demonstrated the validity of this hypothesis quite well.

We have said that just as repentance is the process of the self "dying to itself," so the awareness and acceptance of forgiveness is the experiencing of a "rising again." "The dying and rising again of Christ is the key to the self's possibilities in history," says Reinhold Niebuhr. "All of life is given this norm for the realization of selfhood." [6] And so the cycle is complete: judgment, repentance, and forgiveness signify the eternal dynamics of life, death, and resurrection. "We are treated as . . . dying," Paul told the Corinthians, "and behold we live" (II Cor. 6:8, 9).

We hear many claims that the forgiving community is one in which we should be free to *be* ourselves. As much should be said about the forgiving community being one in which we have the freedom and responsibility to *give* ourselves.

The forgiving community sustains and supports us in our

[5] *Ibid.*
[6] *The Self and the Dramas of History,* p. 66.

pilgrimage. Its investments of faith and hope, as well as material resources, overwhelmingly exceed our ability to repay. Those cognizant of their own indebtedness to the communion of saints do not expect it. They too have experienced grace not of their deserving. How do they begin to repay? By sharing the gift and handing it on to those who look to them for understanding and love.

As a recipient of grace, one cannot just take in grasping self-indulgence as though he deserves it, because then he forfeits any right he has to it. The profligate son, who dissipates his inheritance and gives nothing of himself in return, loses what has been left to him in trust. His childishness and immaturity are under judgment.

The forgiving community, as Emerson points out in another of his hypotheses, is the instrumentality of "realized forgiveness." He regards "realized forgiveness" as connoting the personal awareness of what makes for wholeness. "The Christian fellowship is the instrument that makes real the context of forgiveness." [7] The body of Christ, to which we have referred as *koinonia* and household of God, may not be a particular church but exists wherever there is conscious awareness of God's forgiveness through Christ.

In chapter 10, illustrating the metamorphic stage, I cited the case of Mrs. Wenn. She was finally able to articulate her dread of death, saying she had been unable even to mention the word. She had persistently maintained the physical act of dying held no particular terror for her. Then why, she wondered, should she be so apprehensive of death she could not even talk of it? She granted that probably most people struggled to live and did not wish to die, but she regarded her own fears as bordering on the

[7] *The Dynamics of Forgiveness,* p. 165.

pathological. How, then, was she ultimately released from the paralyzing grip of these fears, attaining sufficient freedom even to minister to a bereaved friend?

Mrs. Wenn's fear of death symbolized her fear of repentance. During the period when she was working through the stage of *reconciliation*, she became aware of the connection. "I just didn't want my old self to die," she exclaimed, laughing at her weakness. "I'm afraid I didn't have faith that a new self could be born. I was skeptical like Nicodemus, I guess," she continued.

She had struggled with her own inconsistency in making demands upon her stepdaughter, while engaging in activities to which she mildly referred as "not altogether moral." She had confessed her sins to a minister at one time. She reported the minister told her God forgives her. "He's worse than I am," she retorted sarcastically, "because I wouldn't forgive anyone like me." She quit attending church for a while, but, since she had been reared in a religious home, she became so guilt-ridden that she decided to give church another try. Yet she was not ready to accept forgiveness, because she had not repented.

What she now saw as her stubborn pride had prevented her from giving up her old divided self to death, experiencing the sorrow and grief which she knew she would feel, and getting new life. One part of her had held tenaciously to a purist self-concept, which she presented as a face to everyone, including her stepdaughter, and even, in some measure, deceptively to herself. Another part of her violated everything her ideal image represented.

As she began to "own" the latter part, by acknowledging it to me, and through becoming more accepting of the weaknesses of others, she became more accepting of herself. As she began to open herself to others, not in lurid confessions, which are another form of indulgence, but in changed attitudes, she discovered the *reality of forgiveness.* "I think it was there all along," she said to me in a follow-up interview several months after we had terminated the counseling relationship. "I just wasn't aware of it."

The household of God performs its proper function if it acts as the forgiving community. It helps the fallen ones to rise again. It never loses hope in them but continues to offer its resources to get them on their way. Thus the forgiving community mediates the redeeming activity of God.

Conclusion

We have affirmed that God's *judgment* is related to his *mercy.* As those persons in counseling who moved into the latter stages of the process of the assimilation of judgment were to testify, the transformation they underwent (through pain and suffering) was definitely perceived as a blessing. They were well aware that the final word is not of judgment but of forgiveness and mercy. Although they have not yet heard the final word, they have experienced enough of its reality to be aware of it.

The "severity" of God's judgment is matched by the "goodness" of His mercy. In the dialogue between the individual and God, this validates itself as the indeterminate possibilities of self-realization and fulfillment of the self's potentialities once it has ceased to seek fulfillment of life from the standpoint of itself. The problem of how the mercy of God is related to His justice is a perpetual problem in the Old Testament. The new Biblical faith of Christianity enters into history with the affirmation that the drama of Christ's life is in fact a final revelation, in which this problem is clarified by the assurance that God takes the demand of His justice upon Himself through Christ's suffering love and therefore, "God was in Christ reconciling the world unto Himself." [8]

As the people in counseling recognized, the judgment of God effects a reconciliation through mercy and forgiveness. They then grasped the meaning of judgment as "the tutor to bring us to Christ," as we may paraphrase a familiar scriptural text (Gal. 3:24). Thus, judgment as law is disciplinary and didactic, prompting men to receive forgiveness, and bringing them to maturity in Christ.

The people who moved into the latter stages of the assimilation of judgment perceived the continuity between God's judgment and his mercy. It was an "aha!" experience for them. No longer did they regard judgment as the absence of God's contingency with their consciousness, but recognized that to be under God's wrath and judgment is to be as truly and existentially related to him as to be under his love and mercy. They learned to recognize that "No" is as personal an address as "Yes."

In the metamorphic stage, the new being is born of the process of assimilation of judgment. The old has passed away. Life is a succession of such births and deaths of the self as its conditions for justification are broken through. Essential to this fulfillment is the assimilation process which produces the new creation. As the body is changed with each act of the assimilation of food, so the self, which incorporates judgment, is transformed. So also is the body of Christ transformed, as it incorporates the judgment of God and receives the gift, in love, of his mercy and forgiveness. Appropriately, therefore, we began this book with the word *judgment*, and we end it with the word *forgiveness*, which is God's final word to man.

[8] Niebuhr, *The Self and the Dramas of History*, pp. 65-66.

SCRIPTURE INDEX

SUBJECT INDEX